MUSLIMS

and the

New World Order

Musa Saleem

I S D S BOOKS

INSTITUTE FOR STRATEGIC AND DEVELOPMENT STUDIES

I S D S BOOKS

Published by **ISDS** BOOKS a division of
INSTITUTE FOR STRATEGIC AND DEVELOPMENT STUDIES
PO BOX 3416
LONDON SW19 8BP
UK

Typesetting, Cover Design and Illustrations by:
The Print Shop
117, Lavender Hill
London SW11 5QL

ISBN 1 898584 00 1

British Library Cataloguing in Publication Data

A catalogue record of this book is available from the British Library.

Printed by: Deluxe Printers, London. Tel: 081-965-1771

بِسْمِ اللهِ الرَّحْمٰنِ الرَّحِيمِ

In the name of Allah, most Gracious, most Merciful

*"... Verily never will Allah change the condition
of a people unless they change
their inner selves... "*

(Surah Raad 13:11)

*'The Search of Knowledge is a sacred
duty imposed upon every Muslim.'*

(Sahih Al-Bukhari: The Book of Knowledge)

'In humility I thank Allah (SWT) for blessing me
with the perfect religion- Al-Islam;
for bestowing me with the finest book
of guidance- the Glorious Qur'an;
for favouring me with the best example
to follow- Prophet Muhammad (SAAS).'

Musa Saleem

Introduction

Islam is a tolerant, balanced and caring religion. It therefore upsets Muslims that the media portrays them as fundamentalists and terrorists when they are nothing more than practising Muslims. Many Muslims are now deeply concerned about the decline of morality, and the economic, environmental and social deterioration of society on a wide front. Muslims believe that their religion and culture provides the solutions to many current dilemmas and afflictions of society. It is these concerns for the current problems and a desire to seek solutions that are the driving forces behind the current Islamic revival.

This Islamic revival is noticeable in almost all countries where Muslims live. In schools, colleges, universities and work places Muslims and Muslimahs feel proud to identify themselves as Muslims. The Islamic renaissance has caused millions of Muslim homes to re-examine their values and way of life. Many are making an effort to lead a life as near as possible by the teachings and ideals of Islam. Furthermore this renewal is now making some inroads among Muslim leaders and decision makers and many princes, princesses, sheikhs and sheikhas. Many non-Muslims are discovering the majesty and wisdom of Islam and are converting to it specially in Europe and America.

With the demise of the Soviet Union a New World Order has descended on earth under the leadership of the United States of America. Some writers and Think Tank specialists predict an armed conflict between the New World Order and the Islamic World Order. We reject this scenario and give our reasons in the article 'The Way Forward'. But first the reader should acquaint himself with Muslims and **real** Islam, with the issues, aims and objectives of this religion specially in relation to Muslim Vs others. It would then be easy to reach some conclusion with a consensus.

The Islamic revival has aroused the curiosity of many and the envy of some. There is no sinister motive behind this revival. Muslims are not planning any revolution, conquest, war or terror either against West or East. In some places Muslims are being oppressed, in others their survival is at risk for no reason other than the fact that they are Muslims. Their revival represents their legitimate aspiration for representative governments in their own lands, their ambition to develop the wealth and resources of their countries and the wish to lead their lives according to the dictates of their religion. In countries where Muslims are in a minority they want nothing more than being left alone to practise their faith, to preserve and maintain their cultural identity and to be treated equally and fairly as law-abiding citizens.

Many non-Muslims wish to know about Islam, some out of curiosity and others with genuine and serious enquiry in mind. They desire to learn about Islam as a religion and as a political, social, financial and cultural system. Some Muslims and non-Muslims are seeking answers to many current issues and problems and want to find out if Islam has any views on the issues and solutions for these problems. Governments, Think Tanks and academics also want to know where Islam is heading and why it is heading there.

An attempt has been made in this book to meet the needs of all these people. It covers a wide range of topics, states clearly the concerns and objectives of the Muslims. It explains why and how they must strive to attain those objectives. The aim of the book is also to establish, with evidence and reasoning that Islam as a religion has no partnership with fundamentalism or terrorism and gives no authority to anyone to commit acts of terrorism in its name or on its behalf. It is disturbing to Muslims that the media often projects an opposite and distorted image of Islam to what this religion actually teaches and preaches.

There is no compulsion in religion and no one has monopoly on knowledge and truth. It is the duty of every human being to seek knowledge and truth. Only then one can know if and what other choices are available.

Musa Saleem
15 Rabi Al-Thani 1414 AH
30 September 1993 AD

NOTES

Allah or God.

Some books and articles on Islam and Muslims use the word 'God', the English translation of the Arabic word 'Allah'. Allah is used in the Qur'an and *hadith* and of course in Arabic religious literature. The word 'God' does not convey the purest concept of either Unity or lack of Gender of the Almighty, because it can be converted to both plural as well as female forms. 'Allah' cannot be so corrupted as the very first essay of this book explains. We have, therefore used 'Allah', throughout this book instead of 'God'.

SWT *Subhanahu-Wa-Tala* means - Glory be to The Most High. Whenever the name of Allah is mentioned in the book this abbreviation has been used as mark of submission and humility.

SAAS stands for *Sallallahu-Alaihi-Wasallam* which means - May the peace and blessings of Allah be upon him. This is used whenever the name Muhammad, Prophet or Messenger is mentioned.

AS stands for *Alaihis-Salaam* which means - On whom be peace. This is used for all the prophets mentioned in the Qur'an - total 25, including Jesus, Moses and Abraham.

RA stands for *Radiallahu Anhu* or *Anha* which means - May Allah be pleased with him or her. It is used whenever the companions or the family of the Prophet is mentioned.

The use of the above abbreviations is recommended. It imparts the modern message of Islam with traditional courtesy and respect.

Quotations from Qur'an.

The quotations from Qur'an are mentioned by the name of Surah - Chapter, followed by the number of the Surah - Chapter which is then followed by the number of the *aya/t* - verse/s. The Qur'an has 114 Surahs and a total of 6666 *ayat*. The numbering of *ayat* in each Surah starts from 1. This should enable any one to check the relevant reference in any Qur'an, in any language, at any time and anywhere in the world. Unlike the Bible the Qur'an does not have new or old testaments , King James or Readers Digest versions. It is the same original book for the past fourteen hundred years with no amendments by any man!

Hadith, traditions of the Prophet (SAAS), has been quoted from Bukhari and Muslim.

Pronunciation of Arabic words.

It is common practice to use diacritical marks for correct pronunciation of Arabic words. We consider that this could be quite misleading as diacritics for some words can vary from one book to another. We have included the meaning of all Arabic words used in this book and avoided diacritics altogether.

Meaning of Arabic Words.

The meaning of Arabic words, generally represented in italics except for widely used words, is given in the footnotes when the word is first encountered.

Contents

The Media and Muslims   1

Jihad and Islam   15

Fundamentalism and Islam   22

Allah (SWT)   27

Allah's Prophets   30

Muhammad (SAAS) - An Example to all Mankind   33

Jesus in Islam   39

Qur'an - Book of Guidance, Wisdom and Comfort   43

Hadith   53

Basic Beliefs and Duties of Muslims   56

Salah   59

Zakah   62

Sawm   66

Hajj & Umrah   70

Duties of Parents to their Children   73

Children's Duties to Parents   76

Islam and the Acquisition of Knowledge   78

The Mosque in Islam   83

Halal and Haram   92

Men in Islam   95

Women in Islam   99

Hijab	105
Islamic System of Morality	110
Islamic Manners toward Parents and Relatives	114
Islamic Behaviour with Neighbours, Friends and Guests	118
Islamic Months	122
The First Four Caliphs	126
Islamic State/Political System	130
The Learned and Islam	144
Islamic Banking, Trade and Investment	148
Islam and Science	153
Islamic Art and Literature	158
Muslim Contribution to Architecture, Mathematics and Morality	160
Islam in Central Asia and Russia	165
Islam in Spain	169
Muslim Countries of the World	172
Islam and some Current Issues	178
The Richest Muslim Country in the World	186
The Development of Muslim Countries	194
Muslim Unity in the midst of Diversity	205
Muhammad's (SAAS) Last Sermon	209
The Way forward	217
ISDS	222

The Media and Muslims

'West fears world-wide havoc from Muslim extremists'

'Sudan   'The Middle East
Jehad'   **Assault Course'**

" The Mosque Militant "

" Islamic Militancy
North Africa's big stick "

"The Islamic Threat"

The above are not clippings from any book or Disney cartoon. They are a very small sample of actual headings, extracted by us from leading newspapers and prestigious news magazines. This is how the media depicts Islam almost on a daily basis to the Western public. But the printed word in newspapers and magazines is not enough for them. An

---

Islam: Submission, resignation, reconciliation to the will of Allah (SWT).

equally distorted view of Islam is being presented in books, on radio and television.

Every Muslim and some non-Muslims who know about Islam and Muslims may wonder as to what the hell is going on. May be the Islam we know it here is different out there. Or may be the boys are really up to something. Others make their views loud and clear that it is nothing but Jewish propaganda on a world-wide scale against Muslims and Islam paid for by some Middle Eastern and African governments with the tacit approval of the leaders of Egypt, Algeria etc. - all cliff hanging on to their power with the fear of a fall any moment straight down the ravine. There are others who believe that all this propaganda against Islam is a sinister plot by the combined resources of the CIA & the State department, MI5 & the Foreign Office, Mossad & the Israeli government.

With such a large number of variables and assumptions, motives and objectives to attack and discredit Islam you might rightly imagine our task being well nigh impossible to cut this Gordian knot and to come up with some ammunition (no guns please, we are Parker pen militants!) to enable Muslims to fight back this falsehood and propaganda against them. The task is difficult but not impossible. We feel pretty annoyed at this unjust media 'tricknology' against Islam and realise the urgent need for Muslims to make every effort to get better press and television coverage.

1. The reasons and motives for the present Western media attack on Islam can be summed up as follows; there is no single reason, it is a combination of reasons.

1.1 The National Interest.

America and Britain could not give a hoot about religion least of all Islam. Their entire planning and action is based on that elusive commodity called our 'National Interest.' They are sincerely and firmly convinced, erroneously of course, that Islam is against their 'National Interest.' If their grandmother was against 'their National Interest' they would probably shoot her.   So their treatment of Islam may be understandable, but not forgivable because it is due to erroneous assumptions and wrong conclusions about Islam and Muslims.

1.2 Media ignorance about the religion called 'Islam'. Most journalists writing about Islam have not taken the trouble to study Islam through its authentic sources - Qur'an, *sunnah* and *seerah*.

1.3 Fear of Islam.

This fear is based on two reasons. If you don't know, you have the fear of the unknown. This fear is less than the fear which is generated in those in positions of power, privilege and authority who have the true knowledge of Islam. They know all about Islam and they know what it will do to their power, privilege and exploitation. The public has nothing to fear from Islam because under Islamic influence with crime rates cut, no interest to pay, little risk of Aids, and much greater law and order, they can only be better off. The same cannot be said about the big money lenders, the rich doing massive tax dodges, politicians fooling the masses in the name of serving them. Don't get us wrong that Islam is an Utopia but it is certainly a lot safer and better system of

---

Sunnah: All the traditions and practices of the Prophet (SAAS) that have become 'models' to be followed by all Muslims.
Seerah: Study of the life of Prophet Muhammad (SAAS).

values and governance. The Western system of democracy, the decline of morality and the cult of the individual has now gone over the top. The philosophy of life that it represents can never lead to a safe and sustainable world. Like the communist system whose inevitable demise came sooner than expected, the time is fast approaching for the demise of the Western system as we know it. We know of no other system than the Islamic system to replace it. Sooner, rather than later Islamic values and ideals will penetrate into Western culture and governments in varying degree. We predict this will happen within twenty five years. If it does not happen and we continue on our present course then disaster on a global scale is not far off. We and those like minded citizens who have concerns about the present and care about the future must make a resolve for the future. As far as we are concerned we herewith declare that we shall wage a relentless war on West and its rotten system-with our Parker pens of course.

1.4   Deliberate propaganda against Islam by Israel and the world Jewry.

The average secular Jew is a civilised and decent fellow. He will not like Islam but he is unlikely to mount a world-wide onslaught against it because it would be against his moral values or he may feel a little guilty for Islam's past favours to his people within the Spanish and Ottoman empires of Muslims. The only real refuge the Jews ever got against centuries of Christian persecution. The same observations are true about the orthodox and ultra-orthodox Jew. Now we come to the Zionist Jew. It is a different ball game here. Their hatred of Islam and Muslims is well known. Their strategic study has convinced them that a perpetual attack on Islam is the best form of their defence. The policies and actions of leaders like Saddam, Gaddaffi and Mubarak have not helped. The Jews have been successful in convincing

America and some other Western powers what a terror Islam is. This has achieved two vital objectives for the Zionist state. It has enabled it to get all the money, material and technology from America and at the same time got it to protect its interests in the world body and to ignore its mischievous activities outside of it. How clever, you might say! Let us admit it, the Jewish people are indeed very clever, sometimes too clever for their own good.

1.5 Deliberate propaganda against Islam mainly by America and Britain and in varying degrees by some other Western countries.

We believe this propaganda against Islam is not due to dislike of Islam as a religion. Many are converting to Islam in these countries. These countries have been led to believe, by a combination of circumstances, that the strengthening of Islam and the establishment of Islamic governments in Africa, Middle East or anywhere else is against their vital 'National Interests'. This belief is so strong that they prefer to support and prop unrepresentative and tyrant governments, against their own ideals of democracy, individual freedom and liberty. A soul destroying exercise for them which they are stomaching and digesting in the name of 'National Interest'.

1.6 Media bashing.

Many journalists and editors maintain very high standards of journalistic integrity and objectivity in reporting on Muslim affairs. Some regretfully are quite the reverse. Islam bashing is saleable news, sells more papers and it is fun to do so. The feeling that I have done my bit for queen and Christianity in attacking Islam is a nice feeling for some morally bankrupt journalists to go home to for the weekend.

2. Techniques and Tactics used in Propaganda against Islam.

There is urgent need for Muslims and others to understand how the West in association with the Jews has been successfully mounting such a campaign and propaganda against Islam and causing such havoc in the Muslim world. At the same time it has also been making a lot of money out of it.

There are nearly 130 Think Tanks in USA, UK and Israel-almost one hundred Think Tanks in Washington alone. Britain has about twenty and Israel about ten. All these countries have various Intelligence services but the most well known on the international scene are the American CIA, the British MI5 and the Israeli Mossad. A number of Think Tanks and large departments in these intelligent services are engaged full-time in research and strategic studies on Islam and Muslims. In fact Washington has more literature on Islam than the largest Muslim library anywhere in the world. Not all Think Tanks or their researchers are against Islam and Muslims nor are all those working in Intelligence services. But the majority is against Islam and they have successfully convinced their leaders that Islam is against the 'National Interests' of their countries. Having been ordered by their leaders to prepare strategic action plans to keep Islam under check these Think Tanks, in co-operation with the intelligence services prepared three distinct techniques to be used against Muslim countries and Muslim leaders. The media was not involved in the preparation of these but it is a full partner in their implementation. The techniques are:

a.   **The ZORO Technique.**
b.   **The BATNA Principle.**
c.   **The TURTLE Tactics.**

What these techniques are and how they have been used and may be used in future is described below.

a. The ZORO Technique.

The Zoro technique is simply to make the chosen adversary look technically and scientifically advanced and his armed forces more powerful than it actually is. If the adversary happens to be a dictator it is easier and more advantageous to do so. The media is selectively fed with false stories of the powerful army, planned atom bomb alias Islamic bomb, chemical warfare capability etc. of the chosen country/ adversary. Everyone in the West and the neighbours of the chosen country/ adversary start getting alarmed. The leaders and his cohorts of this chosen country are, however, over the moon with joy. Their press, radio and television is pouring out the Western stories as confirmation of what their leader has been telling his countrymen all along. The Western stories, although exaggerated, are used by the dictator as proof of his great achievement for his countrymen. This provides him with the excuse to justify all that expenditure of their national wealth. It provides a perfect cover for the dictator and his cohorts to move billions of dollars to Swiss numbered accounts. After sustained propaganda along these lines by Western intelligence and media, the dictator starts believing his own lies.

The next stage of this technique is to lure the leader of the chosen adversary into a trap either by making him an offer he cannot refuse or promising him something that he badly wants but cannot get without Western help or blessing. This is easy to do in a country whose head is a dictator as you only have to fool one man. Impossible under a representative government where issues, priorities and options are discussed and debated. Once the adversary falls for the bait the last phase of this techniques is applied. And that is to finish him off or bring him down to size as the bad guy. It should be noted that the West all along knew that he was a bad guy! It was this technique that was applied against President Saddam Hussain of Iraq, also known in the West as the butcher of Baghdad and the hero of the 'mother of all battles.' On receiving American assurance he was lulled into believing that the Americans would remain neutral if he attacked Kuwait. And so he jumped into the trap and attacked Kuwait. This much is true that the Americans did not care about the Kuwaiti's then or now and they cared about Saddam even less. America and Israel simply wanted Saddam brought down to his knees and to chain the Gulf rulers into permanent dependence on America for security and safety. Just look where Saddam is now and where he has landed his brother rulers in the Gulf. Zoro technique achieved both. America made billions out of it (the war cost the Gulf rulers 200 billion dollars) and passed on a few billion dollars to Israel for services rendered.

b. The BATNA Principle.
This is a powerful negotiating tool also recommended by consultants of Harvard University. But a unique and refined use for this technique has been found by the intelligence services. The technique is simple and highly effective. If you are dealing with three or more parties who have the potential to get united and threaten your 'National Interest' or if you fear one of them could become very strong and may threaten your security what would you do? Naturally you would want to destroy their strength or at least weaken the strength of one or two if not all three. The BATNA Principle enables you to do it without firing a bullet yourself. Successful execution of this technique will not only destroy or weaken your enemy but you will also benefit in the process from it. It is like extracting blood from one or two strong men to build the strength of a stronger man, in this case the instigator of the technique. In the BATNA Principle

you first find the weaknesses of the parties you want to destroy or damage. The greatest weakness of a dictator is his hunger for more power and acceptance. The worst fear of his neighbours is for their security. The BATNA principle involves convincing the dictator that he can have more power and he well deserves it. At the same time you are secretly and in confidence scaring the life out of his neighbours, your presumed friends, by either projecting the dictator himself as a danger to them or some one else in the targeted group who must be sorted out because he is a potential devil and could become a threat to all concerned.   When faced with two potential devils one has little choice except to choose one, make friends with him or at least put up with his machinations.

This was what happened that led Iraq to declare war on Iran. Iran was projected as the devil to the Gulf Arabs about to swallow them. Iraq was presented to them as the lesser devil that could be their saviour. Iraq itself was promised the undisputed leadership of the Arab world if it could help sort out this little problem of Iran for its brother Arabs. Iraq was also promised all the money and killing machines that it needed. President Saddam fell for the BATNA like a bee falls for honey and attacked Iran, Arabs fell for it and dished out billions to their saviour. Gleefully Israel and the West started supplying arms and machinery worth billions of dollars to both Iraq and Iran, all paid in cash and with thanks. While for eight long years Muslim bled Muslim, destroyed each country's industry, commerce, homes and schools. They brought grief and pain to Muslim mothers, wives, sons and daughters until the earth could soak no more Muslim blood and Iraq and Iran hardly had any strength or money left. And all this for nothing! Do we observe tears trickling down some Muslim eyes. It is trickling while we are writing it. But we are not crying for the war, the loss and damage; we are crying for what fools have become leaders of the Muslims - the root cause of such problems. Why blame America, Britain and Israel for Muslim leader's folly. President Saddam Hussain also known in the West as the butcher of Baghdad and the hero of 'mother of all battles' did not become the leader of all Arabs as he was promised. But he did gain the title as 'the most foolish leader of this century.' He fell for both the ZORO technique and the BATNA principle and is sure to be mentioned in the Guinness book of records.

c. The TURTLE Tactics.

This is a deadly tactic and can fool even the cleverest. This technique was specially developed by an Israeli Think Tank for Menachem Begin, the late Israeli prime minister. The sole purpose of this tactics is to keep world opinion in your favour by convincing every body that you are willing, ready and agreeable to negotiate while taking a confidential policy decision to agree to nothing and yield nothing in the proposed negotiations. In brief you do not want to negotiate in your 'National Interest', but want the world to believe that you do. The more the opposition twists and turns the better it is. This technique has been used successfully by Israel against the Palestinians for the last twenty years and could well be used for the next twenty unless a drastic change in fortune takes place in favour of the Palestinians. A modified form of the same technique has been successfully used by Britain, supported by ECC countries and America in Bosnia against the Muslims. In both cases there has been enormous loss of life; terrible atrocities have been committed against women, children and unbelievable suffering inflicted all in the name of 'our National Interest.'

There are also other ways to spread alarm against Islam. The deliberate use of terms like 'Islamic bomb,' 'Islamic fundamentalism,' 'Islamic Jihad' are all part of the same propaganda.

This is how the governments order, the intelligence services and the Think Tanks prepare detailed action plan, the diplomatic services, the media and others deliver to maintain 'our National Interest.'

Readers are reminded that they should master the habit of analysing news items in line with what we have said here. These techniques will be used in future every ten to twenty years because they are an effective tool to keep Muslim and third world countries permanently subservient to Western interests.

There are other motives, reasons and techniques for attacks on Islam some at national and others at international level. But we shall ignore them for the moment. The question now arises what can Muslims, living in the West and facing regular barrage of this unjustified attack on their religion and culture, do about it?

3. Muslims can do something about it.

Neither burning of books or newspapers nor shouting at Speaker's corner will help much. There are formidable forces against Muslims and they have limited resources. The hostility and impotence of some regimes in the Middle East and the misconduct of others on the international arena does not help either. But where there is determination and ingenuity combined with firm faith in the justness of the cause one can always do something about it. Let us examine the options available to Muslims.

3.1 The first rule the Muslims must learn is to play the media game by the existing rules. They cannot deny the reality of their condition. They have got to play the hand they have been dealt and play it as best as they can.

They can write books expounding their cause and pointing out the injustices. It is bound to open the eyes of some. Most humans (Chetnics apart) have some basic decency in them. When they know the truth and are convinced of the merits of the Muslim's grievance on the basis of sound argument and proper reasoning some are bound to say - that is enough. It can be said with confidence that most ordinary Americans and Brits are a lot fairer than many other people on earth. Also they make up their own minds. And among these ordinary citizens there are some formidable individuals worth appealing to.

3.2   Muslim writers and journalists must write, write and write intelligent, articulate and well reasoned articles, letters to the editor, booklets and books to convince the Western readers that:

☛ The struggle by ordinary Muslims in their own countries against corrupt, unrepresentative and tyrant rulers is a struggle for just and representative government. It is neither fundamentalism nor terrorism. The Muslim in his country is waging the same war and carrying on the same struggle which the Americans, the British and the French carried out for their liberty and freedom years ago. True that many Muslim countries became independent from colonial rule but the ordinary citizens never got any freedom. It was usurped by the privileged few.

☛ The only difference between Muslim struggle now and those in the West in the past is that at the end of it the Muslims want Islamic democracy not Western type of democracy. The Islamic system is a tried and tested system of governance which suits the Muslim's temperament and faith. Because this system of government is different it does not mean that it is anti-West or terrorist.

☛ Muslim writers must convince the Western intelligentsia that Islamic government is indeed a better and fairer

Jihad and Islam

One of the most misunderstood words in the West about Muslims and Islam is *jihad*. *Jihad* is an Arabic word which means 'to strive or make effort' or 'to try or exert oneself to one's best ability'. The concept of *jihad* can never be fully understood by its literal meaning, since many Arabic words have far deeper meanings and cannot be substituted by a single English word. In its broader meaning *jihad* can be explained as a continuous struggle and sacrifice by Muslims with their energy, wealth, as well as their life to gain Allah's favour. The Muslims cannot gain Allah's best favours by being wrapped up in some underground bunker or on top of a remote hill, deep in prayer and contemplation, cut off from all humanity. Islam is an active not a passive religion. It requires belief and faith in Allah and His religion as well as active demonstration of these to oneself and to others. This is based on the basic responsibility of a Muslim to practise, preach and establish what is *maruf* (good) and to avoid, warn and defend against what is manifestly *munkar* (bad). It is this internal and external manifestation of the effort and struggle to spread the message of Allah for the pleasure of Allah and as a duty to Allah that is known as *jihad*. Any other struggle or effort by a Muslim in the name of Islam that does not broadly meet this criteria cannot be termed *jihad*.

The persecution and oppression of the weak on earth at the hands of the evil doers is not liked by Allah (SWT). Allah (SWT) does not condone any form of tyranny or violence. A state of tribulation, oppression and persecution is in direct conflict with Allah's (SWT) Commandments in the Qur'an regarding justice, piety and goodness. It is a religious duty of a Muslim to fight against all forms of tyranny and injustice. This fight or struggle can be against an individual, a group or state or any unjust and tyrant ruler.

In all religions and in most nations throughout human history people have struggled and fought against injustice and tyranny. In Islam this fight can be waged by verbal argument and protest, by strike, by the use of pen and media and only in the last resort by armed struggle. Islam has clearly recognised the necessity and importance for such a fight and laid down clear rules of them. Unlike other religions or doctrines Islam is not just a religion but a complete way of life. The Muslim code of conduct is not like any other. Other religions may not provide the rules or may keep neutral in situations where they are confronted with issues of tyranny and oppression. In secular societies religion and politics are kept separate, so the religious sanction and moral deterrent to fight against tyranny and oppression may not be there. In Islam the situation is quite different. A Muslim must stand up against manifest tyranny and oppression by the Commandment of Allah (SWT). Islam has therefore recognised war as a lawful and justifiable course for self defence and for the restoration of peace, freedom and justice. The Qur'anic verse confirms this as follows:

"Fighting is prescribed for you, and you dislike it. But it is possible that you dislike a thing which is good for you, and you love a thing that is bad for you. But Allah knows and you know not."
(Surah Baqara 2:216)

Peace is fundamental and basic to Islam and war comes only as a matter of necessity when there is no alternative course of action. The word 'Islam' means peace and also submission and obedience to the Commands of Allah (SWT). Islam has laid great emphasis to respect human as well as animal life and a Muslim is not allowed to kill any one except for just cause. *Jihad* plays a very important role in Islamic ideology because it encourages constant struggle to eradicate tyranny and vice and to establish justice and virtue. It must be pointed out that all endeavour and all effort in this respect must be for the sake and pleasure of Allah (SWT) alone. There must not be any element, however small, in these efforts, for personal gratification, personal glory or personal gain in any form.

Some believe that Islam encourages and allows forced conversion. This is a great lie against Islam. There is no compulsion and coercion in Islam whatsoever. The concept of freedom of faith in Islam is a Divine Commandment and is abundantly clear. Islam believes that coercion destroys the whole notion of accountability. It is neither right to force one's faith on any one against his will, nor it is practical to do so. Islam does not approve of any action or policy for forced conversion and strongly condemns it. The following verse of the Qur'an refers to this principle:

"Let there be no compulsion in religion: Truth stands out clear from Error; Whoever rejects Evil and believes in Allah has grasped the most trustworthy handhold, that never breaks. And Allah hears and knows all things."
(Surah Baqara 2:256)

The allegation from some prejudiced persons that Muslims are keen on *jihad* to spread Islam is totally without any foundation. The following verse of the Qur'an clearly teaches Muslims how to spread the message of Islam:

"Invite (all) to the Way of your Lord with wisdom and beautiful preaching; and argue with them in ways that are best and most gracious: For your Lord knows best who has strayed from His Path and who receive Guidance."
(Surah Nahl 16:125)

Muslims don't have large scale missionary type institutions. Christians do have them. Billions of dollars are being spent by Christian missionary organisations to buy converts among the poor nations of the world. Even ex-presidents of United States, President Carter for example, are involved actively in missionary work. The fact that Islam has expanded so rapidly in the past and continues to expand even faster now is a credit to the beauty and simplicity of this religion. It is also a testimony to the fact that most people are not so dumb that they cannot distinguish between right and wrong, false and true.

There are two further obligations of *jihad* that must be clearly understood because of their special nature and importance. The one concerns the establishment of just and representative governments in countries where Muslims are in the majority. In such countries any system of government that is not Islamic and not based on the principles of *shari'ah* is the wrong government. The exact administrative form and shape of government is not defined in the Qur'an as this is not the central issue. What is central and obligatory is that such countries where Muslims are in majority must have an Islamic government and must be run by the rules of *shari'ah*. It follows therefore that in running the affairs of such a state Muslims must follow the Divine Commandments concerning justice, Islamic moral values, Islamic interest free system of finance and banking, Islamic welfare system, Islamic equality, accountability and system of consultation. They must also observe the strict Islamic rules to protect, preserve and safeguard the rights of minorities of whatever religion, living within the Islamic state. There is no argument on the validity of these

---

Shari'ah: Islamic law based on Qur'an, *Hadith*, *Ijma* and *Qiyas*.
Ijma: Unanimous consent of the learned men of al-Islam.
Qiyas: One of the foundations of Islamic jurisprudence in which logical reasoning is used by learned Muslims to establish Islamic principles and teachings.

requirements since they are Divine requirements. As to whether the head of such a government is a President, Prime minister, *Khalifa* or *Emir* is for the people or their elected representatives to decide.

An Islamic government is the truest form of 'democratic' government where ultimate power rests with those that are being governed.

Power and authority to the head of such a government is granted on the condition that he will use it for the good of the people within the broad guidelines of Divine law as laid down by Allah (SWT) and His Messenger. The head of such a government is accountable to both the people and to Allah (SWT). The ultimate sovereignty of such a state is vested in Allah (SWT), the head of state and his ministers exercise this authority in His name.

It is the duty of every Muslim in Muslim majority countries to ensure the establishment of just and representative Islamic governments and to wage the necessary *jihad* for it. This is not a struggle against the interests of West or East, or struggle for personal glory or benefit but the religious duty of the Muslim to do so on the broad principle laid down for him to forbid evil and promote virtue, to eradicate injustice and tyranny and replace it with justice and security. The Western media has branded this struggle for good government by ordinary Muslims in their own countries as terrorism. Amazing, how one can twist and turn fact to fiction, truth to falsehood simply because they don't fit in with one's own erroneous ideas and perceptions or 'the National Interests' of one's country.

It should be clear that the Islamic form of government briefly outlined above is the only suitable system of government for Muslim countries. The Parliamentary system as is the case in the United Kingdom or the Presidential system of the United States are neither suitable nor superior systems for Muslim countries.

"You are the best of people evolved from mankind. You enjoin what is right and forbid what is wrong and you believe in Allah..."
(Surah Al-i-Imran 3:110)

"Thus We have made you a people justly balanced (of the middle path) so that you could be witnesses over nations ..."
(Surah Baqara 2:143)

The other *jihad* obligation on every Muslim is to convey the true message of Allah (SWT) to every non-Muslim with the object that they also will freely choose the path of Islam. Muslims are notoriously casual about preaching or spreading the word of Allah (SWT) in comparison to the conscientious manner the Catholics, Evangelists and Jehova witnesses carry out this task. Even the Jews, never renowned for serious preaching and conversion, seem to be taking on this task rather seriously lately. Just look out for the religious stall at Tel Aviv airport departure lounge next time you are passing through Israel.

The following Surah from the Qur'an is worth reflecting by both Muslims and non-Muslims. They provide the guideline to Muslims for their relations with the people of the book.

"And dispute you not with the People of the Book (Jews and Christians) except with means better (than mere disputation), unless it be with those of them who inflict wrong (and injury): But say 'We believe in the Revelation which has come down to us and in that which came down to you; our Allah and your God is One, and it is to Him we bow (in Islam)."
(Surah Ankabuut 29:46)

What is meant here by means better than mere disputations? It is that Muslims must seek true common grounds of belief and must show by their urbanity, kindness, sincerity, truth and genuine anxiety their desire to exert themselves for the good of others. The ordinary Muslims struggling for this cause are not cranks seeking selfish and questionable objectives but are true believers and practitioners of Islam.

We can summarise *jihad* by saying that to a Muslim *jihad* is Islamic monasticism. It is continuous till the day of judgement. There is no respite from it. *Jihad* is based on three pillars. Firstly, intensification of Islam in oneself and eradication of evil. Secondly, spreading the word of Allah (SWT) to all corners of the world by wisdom and advice. Thirdly, *jihad* is military preparedness to repel aggression and readiness to die willingly for Allah (SWT).

Fundamentalism and Islam

Encyclopaedia Britannica 1985 'edition' devotes almost two pages to the term 'Fundamentalism'. It defines fundamentalism as a conservative movement in American Protestantism arising out of the millenarian movement of the 19th century and emphasising as fundamental to Christianity the literal interpretation and absolute inerracy of the Scriptures, the imminent and physical second coming of Christ, the Virgin Birth etc. It goes on to say that there are a series of Organisations for Fundamentalists paralleling the professional and business organisations of American Society.

Nowhere in the above Britannica is there any mention of Islam v Fundamentalism or Fundamentalists. Not even under its very comprehensive and well researched articles on Islam to which many pages have been allocated.

The Oxford dictionary defines Fundamentalism as the belief that the Bible is literally true and should form the basis of religious thought and practice.

The Muslim Holy books - Qur'an and *hadith* make no mention of Fundamentalism or Fundamentalists either in the original Arabic or in any authentic translations. Muslim religious literature has no mention or discussion of fundamentalism in either *tafseer* (scholarly explanations of Qur'an) or in the explanation of *ahadith.*

The citizens of the West whether Muslim or non - Muslim are receiving daily rations of the word 'Islamic Fundamentalists' in newspapers, magazines, books, radio and television. This is reported in such a negative manner that the reader may start to believe, after such exposure, that there is something odd and sinister about Islam and Muslims.

Believe us dear reader that there is nothing sinister about

Hadith/Ahadith (pl.):   Sayings and actions of the Prophet (SAAS) based on authentic reports.

Islam. The only thing odd about Islam is its total lack of any oddity. It appears that there is an altogether different reason for this propaganda. Islam is a good religion; its teachings offer solutions to many of our current problems; it brings down to size all those high and mighty kings, politicians, popes and priests, bankers and lenders, and the very privileged individuals; it offers to all its true followers rich and poor an inner peace and a balanced, way of life that we all long for. It is no wonder that this propaganda against Islam is being waged by a small and influential lobby with their vested interest in maintaining the status quo. They are worried that if Islam reaches the ordinary masses and the intellectuals in the West or East their own game of mass exploitation will be blown to smithereens.

This propaganda is media 'tricknology' at its best. It is also being carried out by a small but influential group of writers and journalists whose very livelihood may be at stake if they do not do it or who have other motives in such attacks. These writers and journalists have said good-bye to intellectual integrity and journalistic fairness.

We quote below some verses from the teachings of Qur'an, which clearly establish the basic postulates of Islam.

No compulsion in religion.

"Let there be no compulsion in religion: Truth stands out Clear from Error..."
(Surah Baqara 2:256)

Good Deeds.

"By (the token of) Time (through the Ages), Verily man is in loss, Except such as have Faith, and do righteous deeds, And (join together) in the mutual teaching of Truth, and of Patience and Constancy."
(Surah Al-Asr 103:1-3)

Justice.

"Allah commands justice, the doing of good , and liberality to kith and kin, and He forbids all shameful deeds, and injustice and rebellion: He instructs you, that you may receive admonition."
(Surah Nahl 16:90)

"Allah orders that you return trusts to their owners and that if you judge between people, you judge justly..."
(Surah Nissa 4:58)

"O you who believe! Be firm in justice as witness for Allah, even in cases against yourselves, your parents and your kin..."
(Surah Nissa 4:135)

Unity, Variety, Virtue and Piety.

"and among Allah's signs are the creation of heavens and the earth, and the variation in your languages and your colours, truly in that are signs for those who know."
(Surah Ruum 30:22)

"O mankind! We created you from a single (pair) of a male and a female, and made you into nations and tribes, that you may know each other. Indeed the noblest among you in the sight of Allah is the one who is the most righteous of you ."
(Surah Hujuraat 49:13)

Permission to fight for self defence.

"Permission (to fight) is given to those against whom war is being wrongfully waged and verily , Allah has indeed the power to Succour them: those who have been driven from their homelands against all right for no other reason than their saying. 'Our Lord and Sustainer is Allah'!..."
(Surah Hajj 22:39-40)

The above verses from the Qur'an are only a small sample that show the balance, moderation, virtue, tenderness, logic, justice and everlasting wisdom of Islam for the guidance of all mankind.   There is no element of fundamentalism, terrorism or intolerance in these verses. These are some of the basic Qur'anic teachings. Faith in and practice of these teachings makes one   a better Muslim. These verses   are only a small part of the foundation and structure of the religion called Islam. Most Muslims practice the basic tenets of their faith.   Those who do not are not practising Muslims.   Those who do not believe in the basic teachings of their religion nor practice it cannot be regarded as Muslims and are not part of the Muslim community.

In addition to the propaganda of fundamentalism both Islam and Muslims are also being attacked for terrorism.

The menace of terrorism today; individual, group or state, can hardly be blamed on any religion.   The origins and root causes of most of the terrorism are social and political injustice; economic, cultural, and physical tyranny; the exploitation of poor nations by rich nations; denial of just and free governments to people; propping up of tyrant and unrepresentative rulers by some richer nations because of their 'National Interest'.   Any terrorism, including state terrorism carried out for political or other objectives cannot be blamed on religion.

Islam forbids all forms of terror and tyranny particularly

towards innocent people. It further forbids, even in war, any unjust or cruel treatment of women, children and elderly persons; deliberate destruction of livestock and environment as well as cruelty towards the defeated enemy. Not only this, it commands Muslims and all those who have compassion and sense of justice to stand up and fight against tyranny and injustice.

"...And Allah means no injustice to any of His creatures."
(Surah Al-i-Imran 3:108)

That the current media propaganda is manifestly unfair to Islam will become clear from the following example. Israel has a sizeable ultra-orthodox Jewish population. Many of them live in and around Jerusalem. These very strict and observant Jews are also in UK and the United States. On religious issues they have been known to make violent protests including burning and stoning of cars and torching their own mayor. All this in the name of religion. But no one ever labels them as fundamentalists. Bearded, unusually dressed and strictly observant the orthodox Jews do not look much different from the bearded, unusually dressed strictly observant Muslims. In seeking to impose their views, sometimes violently, the former is labelled as orthodox while struggling to establish a just and representative government and fighting tyranny the latter is labelled as a fundamentalist/ terrorist. It is no wonder that the average Muslim believes that the press is hostile and unfair to Islam and is possibly controlled by anti-Muslim Jews and Christians.

We hope that writers, journalists and editors of integrity will re - examine their attitude to Islam and Muslims. Their current stance is causing harm and injury to innocent, ordinary Muslims. It is helping to prop up many tyrant rulers in Muslim countries. And it is encouraging non-Muslim majority in some Muslim minority countries to commit acts of injustice and cruelty against fellow Muslims.

Allah (SWT)

Muslims are monotheists. A monotheist is one who firmly believes that there is only one God - henceforth referred to in this book by the Arabic name Allah (SWT). The name Allah (SWT) is unique since it is neither male nor female, and it cannot be converted into a plural form; while the word God can be changed into Gods and Goddesses or (gods and goddesses). The concept of monotheism or *Tawhid* in Arabic is the very root and foundation of a Muslim's belief. No adulteration of any form is possible here. What is more, unless one believes in it one cannot even commence one's journey on the Islamic road. Why has Islam laid such great emphasis on the Unity of Allah (SWT)? Judaism and Christianity, older religions than Islam, corrupted this belief in the Unity of Allah (SWT). In Christianity the basic concept of Unity was not only reversed to Trinity but Allah (SWT) was also made into a family person. According to the Qur'an no new religion will be established by Allah (SWT) until the Day of Judgement. Because of this so much emphasis has been placed on the Unity of the Lord in Islam, the last revealed religion perfected by Divine Commandment.

Faith in the Unity of Allah (SWT) is:

I. Unity of Lordship:
The belief that there is only one Lord for the universe and that is Allah (SWT).

II. Unity of Worship:
The belief that none has the right to be worshipped except Allah (SWT).

Islam: Complete submission or resignation to the Will of Allah (SWT).
Muslim: One who completely submits to the Will of Allah (SWT).

III. Unity of the Names and the Qualities of Allah (SWT).

The belief that we must not name or qualify Allah except with what He or His Messenger (SAAS) has named or Qualified Him.

The Qur'an mentions ninety-nine names of Allah (SWT), each name is connected with one of His virtues and related to some aspect of the life of man. When a man is given a name which relates to one of the Ninety-nine Names of Allah (SWT), it should be preceded by *Abd* (servant of).

Allah (SWT) hears what is in a person's heart. Whether one speaks aloud or have silent words for Allah (SWT), there is no difference, for He knows what is in our hearts. The beginning of the straight path is with Allah (SWT). The journey through it is with Allah (SWT). At the end of this path is Allah (SWT). That which leads people to disaster is to forget Allah (SWT). The tongue may utter *dhikr* (mention and remembrance of Allah), but it is the heart that feels and confirms it.

The Messenger (SAAS) of Allah (SWT) has said: 'There is a piece of flesh in the body. If it is sound, the entire body is sound. If it is unsound, the entire body is unsound. It is the heart!'

A Muslim's heart that does not have absolute faith in and obedience to Allah (SWT) and love for His Prophet (SAAS) can never be sound. No amount of exercise in the gym, heart surgery or heart by-pass can be of much use to such a person.

The Qur'an is full with the praise, wisdom, mercy, virtues and qualities of Allah (SWT). The following are just two examples:

"Say: He is Allah, The One and Only; Allah the Eternal, Absolute; He begetteth not, nor is He begotten; and there is none Like unto Him."
(Surah Ikhlas 112:1-4)

"Allah! There is no god but He, the Living, the Self-subsisting, Eternal. No slumber can seize Him nor sleep. His are all things in the heavens and earth. Who is there to intercede in His presence except with His leave? He knows what (appears to His creatures as) Before or After or Behind them. Nor they can attain anything of His knowledge except that He wills them to attain. His dominion extends over the heavens and the earth, and He feels no fatigue in guarding and preserving them; for He is the Most High, the Supreme (in glory).
Let there be no compulsion in religion;
Truth stands out Clear from Error... "
(Surah Baqara 2:255-256)

Allah (SWT) in His divine mercy may pardon all sins. But the sin of *Shirk*, i.e., associating partners with Him will never be pardoned. This is understandable. If we accept another sovereign in authority in UK in addition to or in competition with HM the Queen we shall be charged with treason and accordingly punished. And the Queen is just a mortal head of one country. Just imagine how upset the Lord of the Universe, with so much more power than any king or queen must feel if anyone dare associate others to share His Sovereignty!

Shirk: Idolatory, paganism. To worship others along with Allah (SWT).

Allah's Prophets

Allah (SWT) has sent his prophets, since the beginning of Creation, for the guidance of man.

No human being can acquire learning entirely on his own. When we are children, we depend on our parents to teach us. As we grow older we learn from relatives, teachers and fellow human beings.

One can only attain the high standards of moral character, good behaviour and correct guidance to lead a proper life from those who possess these qualities. And those who teach us must have learnt from similar sources themselves. Following this chain of learning and guidance we reach the ultimate source of guidance - Allah (SWT). Between man and Allah (SWT) are the prophets specially chosen from among men by Allah (SWT) to teach and guide man, His very special Creation.

The right and proper way for man is to live according to the teachings of Allah (SWT) and in absolute obedience to Him and His laws. Allah (SWT) has decreed that man should obtain this knowledge from His prophets, also known as Messengers of (Allah). The chosen prophets were commanded by Allah (SWT) to convey His message and show the right path to other human beings. Messengers were chosen by Allah (SWT) from among ordinary people. The prophets lived ordinary lives like all mortal human beings; they married, had families, experienced the ebb and flow of life and endured great hardships for the pleasure of Allah (SWT).

Among the people a misconception arose that prophets had special powers to change the fate and destinies of people. They also thought that prophets were masters of good and evil and could harm or reward fellow human beings. No prophet possessed any special power or miracle except what Allah (SWT) granted him. Some prophets did perform miracles but it was under Allah's authority and with His permission. The Qur'an has confirmed this powerlessness of Messengers of Allah (SWT) and emphasised the fact that Messengers were ordinary people. Their honour and dignity was in their obedience to Allah (SWT) and their determination and courage against hostility and hardship to convey the message of Allah (SWT) to the people.

According to a saying attributed to Prophet Muhammad (SAAS), the number of prophets sent by Allah (SWT) is one hundred and twenty-four thousand. However, the Qur'an only mentions twenty-five prophets. Jesus - Isa (AS) is acknowledged as a prophet in the Qur'an. It is the Christian people that turned him into god, god's son and added insult to injury by proclaiming that he died in atonement of their sins. How can one mortal man be held responsible for the terrible sins committed by so many in the past and still being committed? Hitler and Stalin, just two men among many and both Christians in their early lives committed enormous atrocities and sins against fellow human beings. It is difficult to believe that any atonement through anyone is possible or justifiable for them. And if our conclusion is incorrect then the Al-Capone's and Ivan the Terrible's of this world will have the very best here and also over there. Vice and virtue, crime and punishment will then be just hollow words.

The first prophet was Adam (AS). The last Prophet is Muhammad (SAAS). There will be no more prophets because Allah's (SWT) guidance to mankind which began with Adam (AS) was completed by Prophet Muhammad (SAAS).

Among the most famous prophets are Ibrahim (AS), biblical name Abraham; Musa (AS), biblical name Moses; Isa (AS), biblical name Jesus. The last, most famous and exalted of them all is Prophet Muhammad (SAAS). As

Muslims we must believe in all the prophets and Messengers of Allah (SWT). Whenever any prophet's name is mentioned Muslims should add - *Alaihis-Salaam* (AS), which means 'on him be peace.' Whenever the Prophet Muhammad's name is mentioned Muslims must add - *Sallallahu Alaihi Wa Sallam* (SAAS), which means 'may the peace and blessings of Allah (SWT) be upon him.'

Muhammad (SAAS)
An Example to all Mankind

In his book 'The 100 - A Ranking of the Most Influential Persons in History', Michael H. Hart, an American author ranks Muhammad (SAAS) as **'number one'** followed by ninety-nine others of our world's most distinguished persons since the beginning of time.

All qualities desirable in a man have been perfected in the person of Muhammad (SAAS) by Allah (SWT). His achievements in his lifetime are far beyond anything ever achieved by any man. His lasting legacy and example in all areas of moral, spiritual and practical life are unmatchable. So much so that the Qur'an itself says about him as follows:

"And thou (standest) on an exalted standard of character."
(Surah Qalam 68:4)

"You have indeed in the Apostle of Allah a beautiful pattern of conduct..."
(Surah Ahzab 33:21)

Thousands of books have been written on the life and achievements of Muhammad (SAAS) in the last fourteen hundred years and they are still being written. One set of books alone, contains seven volumes of over six thousand pages - 'Encyclopaedia of Seerah by the Seerah Foundation.' These books show how every area of human existence and endeavour has been touched and influenced by the last Prophet (SAAS) of Allah (SWT). Details of his life and achievements from birth to death are available in simple books for young children and in serious books for learned readers.

A brief summary of the evidence that confirm why he is a model to all mankind is given below.

1. Example as a Person.

1.1 As a Boy.

The Prophet (SAAS) is a perfect example for all young people who need someone as a role model to follow. He was well behaved, gentle, noble and of spotless character. He kept himself in his youth totally free from any obscenity and indecency. As a young boy he tended the sick, was considerate to his neighbours, respectful to the old, ready to help the widowed, orphaned and infirm. His integrity and truthfulness so impressed his people that they called him *As-Sadiq* (the Truthful) and *Al-Ameen* (the Trusted).

1.2 As an Adult.

When at the age of forty the Prophet (SAAS) started preaching the religion of Islam most Makkans opposed his mission. But they still had complete confidence in his integrity and truthfulness and used to deposit their valuables with him. This proves the very high standard of his character.

Muhammad (SAAS) never practised idol worship even before his Prophet-hood as was the common practice of pagan Makkans before they accepted Islam. He never committed any such act that could blemish his character. There is no person in history who has displayed such exalted standards of personal conduct and character throughout childhood and as an adult, both before and after Prophet-hood. They all had some weakness; some lacked qualities of justice and fairness, others were deficient in kindness and modesty. The Prophet lived a happy, balanced life and was a perfect example as a husband, father, family member, friend and neighbour.

2. Other Personal Qualities.

If anyone exceeds in the following selected areas of qualities and attains a very high level of conduct then such a man can be regarded as a model. The Prophet (SAAS) excelled in these qualities far beyond what can be reasonably expected from any man.

Love, Mercy, Generosity, Forgiveness, Hospitality, Sacrifice, Simplicity, Humility, Modesty, Sincerity, Integrity, Truthfulness, Justice, Fair Dealing, Fulfilment of Promises and Keeping of Trust, Piety, Righteousness, Perseverance in Adversity, Courage and Bravery in battle and danger, Magnanimity in Victory, Politeness and Kindness.

In all the above areas there is no equal to the Prophet's (SAAS) life example.

3. Special Qualities and Attributes of the Prophet.

3.1   He was a superb Messenger, teacher and commentator of Qur'an. His life was living Qur'an both in his *sunnah* (all the traditions and practices of the Prophet (SAAS) that have become as 'models' to be followed by all Muslims), and his *ahadith* (sayings and actions of the Prophet (SAAS) based on authentic reports).

3.2   He was a great leader and guide both during the early Muslim hardship and adversity and at the time of Muslim conquest and prosperity. Throughout he displayed unshakeable faith in Allah (SWT) and in his mission.

3.3   He was the first ruler of an Islamic State that called upon his qualities as an administrator, legislator, judge and military commander. He met this challenge admirably.

3.4   He had no thirst for power either for show or misuse. Even as head of state and religious leader with enormous power and authority he lived the life of a very ordinary citizen absorbed in piety and prayer and without any pomp and ceremony. There is no known example of any such person in human history.

4.　His Legacy.

4.1　He left the legacy of a perfected religion - Islam - which spread in his lifetime to the whole of Arabia and within a short time after his death to a large part of the world.　Today his *Ummah* is over one thousand million strong and his message　more universal and relevant now than at any time in　history.

4.2　He left the legacy of an authentic and unadulterated Divine Book of guidance - the Qur'an, his *sunnah* and *ahadith*　which together provide complete and clear guidance to every person in all his needs whether they are in the spiritual, social, cultural, political, economic or whatever area.

4.3　He left a permanent legacy for us:

✓　**To believe in one Allah (SWT) and His last Messenger.**

✓　**To believe and respect all Allah's Prophets.**

✓　**To enjoin what is good and forbid what is evil.**

✓　**To lead a balanced natural life morally, physically and spiritually avoiding all　extremes.**

✓　**To believe in the equality of all human beings with no distinction of race, colour or origin.**

Ummah:　A nation, a people, a sect. Usually refers to Muslim community.

✓ To believe that there is no compulsion in religion.

✓ To practice *taqwa* and to fight tyranny and injustice.

5.   What others say about Muhammad (SAAS) and the religion that he preached?

Below are just a few examples from the vast tributes made by non - Muslims to Muhammad (SAAS).

'Head of State as well as the Church, he was Caesar and Pope in one; but, he was Pope without the Pope's pretensions, and Caesar without the legions of Caesar, without a standing army, without a bodyguard, without a police force, without a fixed revenue. If ever a man had the right to say that he ruled by a right divine, it was Muhammad, for he had all the powers without their support. He cared not for the dressings of power. The simplicity of his private life was in keeping with his public life.'   **(Reverend Bosworth Smith)**

'Circumstances changed, but the Prophet of God did not. In victory or in defeat, in power or in adversity, in affluence or in indigence, he was the same man, disclosed the same character. Like all the ways and laws of God, Prophets of God are unchangeable.'

(Professor K.S. Ramakrishna Rao)

'If greatness of purpose,
smallness of means
and astounding results
are the three criteria of human genius, who could dare to compare any great man in modern history with Muhammed?

The most famous men created arms, laws and empires only. They founded if anything at all, no more than material

---

Taqwa: Purity, abstinence, fear of Allah (SWT), piety, righteousness.

powers which often crumbled away before their eyes. This man Muhammed moved not only armies, legislations, empires, peoples and dynasties, but millions of men; and more than that he moved the altars, the gods, the religions, the ideas, the beliefs and souls.

On the basis of a Book, every letter of which has become law, he created a spiritual nationality which blended together peoples of every tongue and of every race.....

The idea of the unity of God, proclaimed amidst the exhaustion of fabulous theologies, was in itself such a miracle that upon its utterance from his lips it destroyed all the ancient superstitions...

His endless prayers, his mystic conversations with God, his death and his triumph after death; all these attest not to an imposture but to a firm conviction which gave him the power to restore a dogma. This dogma was twofold, **the unity of God and the immateriality of God;** the former telling what God is, the latter telling what God is not....

.... "PHILOSOPHER, ORATOR, APOSTLE, LEGISLATOR, WARRIOR, CONQUEROR OF IDEAS, RESTORER OF RATIONAL BELIEFS, of a cult without images; the founder of twenty terrestrial empires and one spiritual empire, that is Muhammed. **AS REGARDS ALL STANDARDS BY WHICH HUMAN GREATNESS MAY BE MEASURED, WE MAY WELL ASK, IS THERE ANY MAN GREATER THAN HE?"**
(Lamartine, Historie de la Turquie, Paris 1854, Vol. II pp. 276 - 277)

It is no wonder that Allah (SWT) says in the Qur'an, referring to Muhammad (SAAS):

"Verily those who plight their fealty to thee do no less than plight their fealty to Allah,..."
(Surah Fatah 48:10)

Jesus in Islam

Some non-Muslim readers may wonder why we have included Jesus (AS) in a book about Islam and Muslims. This is for two reasons. Firstly because Jesus-Arabic name Isa (AS) is considered a prophet in Islam. And secondly he is mentioned in the Qur'an in some detail. His birth, death and family are all detailed in Qur'anic verses. Many Christians do not know that Muslims must not only believe in Jesus but by Divine Commandment they must respect and honour him as one of the Messengers of Allah (SWT). Both Muslims and Christians agree on the miraculous birth of Jesus. But beyond this they part company. In this brief article it is this common belief in Jesus's birth by the two largest religions in the world and the basic disagreement on all else connected with him that we shall discuss. For a Muslim the worst sin in the sight of Allah (SWT) is to associate a partner or family to Him. Jesus is therefore of special interest to Muslims and an intellectual challenge to them to peruse and investigate the issues concerning Jesus as to what made the Christians regard Jesus as son of God and a god, and to believe in Jesus's alleged crucification as perennial atonement for their sins.

Birth of Jesus.

Jesus was born without a human father. This led Christians to designate him as the son of God. But to a Muslim this appears to be highly illogical. Allah (SWT) created Adam (AS) without father and mother followed by Eve (AS) and then millions of humans were born from the normal union of man and woman as the progeny of Adam (AS) and Eve (AS). Jesus's birth without a father has simply reaffirmed Allah's powers of creation already demonstrated in the case of Adam (AS) and Eve (AS). If the title son of God is appropriate then it must go to Adam (AS) first and not to Jesus (AS).

Atonement of sin by Jesus and the making of Jesus into a son of God.

Atonement (noun) is from the verb 'atone' which means act in a way that compensates for a previous wrong. By atonement the Christians mean the suffering and death of Christ (Jesus) to atone for the sins of mankind - past, present and future. In other words it means the propiation of God by the expiation of the sacrificial death of Jesus (AS) for mankind's sins. To any intelligent and reasonable mind this must be one of the most difficult propositions to swallow. We make the following observations:

a. To make a third party responsible for the actions of someone is against the very notions of justice and accountability. Even our laws do not recognise this principle. A father cannot be punished for the murder committed by his son nor a wife is responsible for the criminal acts of her husband. This principle is well established in all nations.

b. Most Christians believe that God Himself took human form as Jesus. Why would God, Who is capable of creating the Universe and human beings according to the same Christians, should come to earth in Jesus's mortal body, be insulted, beaten and suffer other indignities and then die for the salvation of the very people who were inflicting on him such insults and abuse. As an Al-Mighty God He should be quite capable of forgiving, punishing and rewarding His subjects according to their deeds. Why should He suffer such indignities Himself which neither demonstrates His Al-Mightiness nor His intelligence?

c. Punishment and reward even in our society are proportional to the severity of the crime committed or the degree of good done. If one commits murder one will either be hanged or receive life imprisonment. Similarly ordinary acts of public good may be rewarded with an OBE while the doing of greater good or service might earn a knighthood. So far it seems logical and reasonable. The alleged death of Jesus on the cross was not unusual in those days. Dying on the cross was the usual form of Roman punishment for the carrying out of death penalty just as electric shock, gas chamber or putting to the sword is in our time. Thousands of people were dying this way during Roman rule; nothing exceptional or extraordinary in Jesus's death. How can this one death atone for all our sins when thousands of heroes have died since then, some much more horrible and painful deaths than Jesus. These heroes died in the cause of liberty, in their fight against tyranny and for their belief in one Lord, often on behalf of their fellow human beings. Surely they should all be granted the same status as Jesus. It seems grossly unfair that for three years of work (total period of Jesus ministry) and for three days of suffering (alleged maximum time for his death) Jesus (AS) should be so exalted and others so forgotten. No one with any sense of justice or common sense will accept this.

d. Both Christians and Muslims agree that their God / Allah (SWT) is a Lord of mercy, justice and compassion. Jesus came to spread His message and guide His creation. He was not only innocent of any crime but most deserving of God's help and mercy. God showed His mercy and gave His help to all His Messengers. Why would God want to inflict this alleged cruel and humiliating crucifixion on His favourite servant and Messenger? This does not reflect God's justice, mercy, love and forgiveness. In fact this makes God look very unjust.

From the above it is clear to the Muslim that something somewhere is very wrong in Christian ideas about Jesus. The Muslim position regarding Jesus covering all the above matters are given in the Qur'an very clearly. They can be summarised as follows:

1. Jesus (AS) was born to Mary - *Mariam* (AS) in Arabic - without a father on Allah's Command.

2. Jesus (AS) acted as a Messenger of Allah to spread His true message which by then was being misinterpreted and abused by the Jews.

3. Jesus was not crucified but raised to heaven by Allah (SWT).

4. Islam rejects the doctrine of crucification, the concept of atonement and the belief that Jesus (AS) was son of God. Muslims believe that these beliefs are against common sense, logic and are manifestly unfair and absurd.

5. Muslims believe that the greatness of Jesus arises from the fact that he was chosen by Allah (SWT) as His Messenger; blessed with revelation to spread His message. It is an act of faith for Muslims to believe in Jesus (AS), to respect and honour him as Allah's (SWT) Messenger and Prophet.

Qur'an - Book of Guidance, Wisdom and Comfort

In mid 1993 a secular Turkish journalist made the statement that the Qur'an was over 1000 years old and thus not suitable for Turks to follow it in modern times. Salman Rushdie did his bit to insult not only the Qur'an but the Prophet (SAAS), his family and the entire *Ummah*.

Our investigations have revealed that neither the Turkish journalist nor Salman Rushdie know a word of Arabic so they could not have read the book to justify the comments they made.

If a man who did not know and could not understand the English language had expressed similar views on Shakespeare or Shelley or someone who did not know and could not understand French had spoken in similar terms about Proust or Maupassant he would be termed 'nuts' by the general public and totally rejected by the literary circle. Not for the criticism which he has the right to make but for his qualifications to do it. This of course is for books written by man for the amusement, entertainment and some instruction of his fellow men. Imagine how 1000 million Muslims should feel about such unjust criticism of Qur'an, a Divine book revealed by Allah (SWT) whose authenticity is not questioned by many even in the non-Muslim camp. It is no wonder Muslims think that Salman Rushdie is a sick man. And some of them would like to cure him if he ever comes out of his shell.

What is this book called Qur'an? We all know that it is the Muslim Holy Book and Allah's (SWT) word and a book of guidance. But some may want better explanation as to

---

Ummah: A nation, a people, a sect. Usually refers to Muslim community.

what exactly is in this book for which vast number of Muslims have such love and reverence.

The Qur'an is the Creator's greatest blessing to mankind. If one truly believes in the Creator and His Creation then he must believe in His Book. If one does not believe in Him then one cannot have faith in His Book.

❖ The Qur'an is **guidance** (*hudan*) and **light** (*nur*) which shows its readers and followers the way through darkness.

❖ The Qur'an is the **criterion** (*furqan*) that distinguishes between truth and falsehood.

❖ It is the **balance** (*mizan*) in which things are weighed to establish their veracity or falsity.

❖ It is **healing** (*shifa*). The medicines cure our body ills. This medicine cures both social sickness as well as the sickness of the inner self - soul.

❖ It is a constant **reminder** (*dhikr*). It reminds us why we are here; where is our destiny; what are our duties; which actions are proper and which are improper; how to conduct ourselves in our daily life; what are the rewards and punishments for our actions both here and the Hereafter.

So much in just one book! Surely not possible some might say. There are two ways to find this out. Firstly by studying the book preferably in its original language. Secondly the Qur'an itself makes some claims worth contemplating:

"A book We have sent down to you, full of blessings, that men of understanding may ponder its signs, and so remember."
(Surah Saad 38:29)

"And if you are in any doubt whether it is We who have revealed this Book to Our servant, then produce just a Surah like it and call all your supporters and seek in it the support of all others save Allah. Accomplish this if you are truthful."
(Surah Baqara 2:23)

Fourteen hundred years have passed since the above *aya* was revealed. So far this challenge has still not been met.

Addressing the Prophet (SAAS) who was an unlettered man, the Qur'an proves that it is none other than Allah's words in the following verse.

"And thou was not able to recite a Book before this (Book came), nor are thou able to transcribe it with thy right hand: In that case, indeed, would the talkers of vanities have doubted."
(Surah Ankabuut 29:48)

It is not difficult but impossible for any man who can neither read nor write to read and explain Shakespeare let alone write it. How could Muhammad (SAAS) an unlettered mortal author Qur'an, as some cynics in the past have suggested, insults one's imagination and makes a mockery of intelligence and common sense.

The above is some of the evidence for the authenticity, beauty and scholarship of the Qur'an as well as its universal

---

Aya/t: Verse/verses of the Qur'an. Means signs, proofs, clear evidence or miracles.

message. Now the question is how can Muslims and indeed others get the most benefit from this book of Guidance. An ordinary book of a student, in the course of his studies, makes some demands on him to grant any benefit. He has to study the book, understand it, believe in its accuracy, practice its sums, grammar or whatever, look into the explanations of teachers or the answer book. And all this is needed just to understand the subject matter or pass the examination. It is only natural that a book like Qur'an containing much more knowledge and wisdom must make some demands for its benefits to be showered. It does indeed do so.

The Qur'an makes five demands on every Muslim. These are:-

1. A Muslim is required to believe in it.
Without faith in the authenticity and wisdom of what you are reading you can hardly expect to get any benefit from it. When one reads Shakespeare one believes he is reading the genuine stuff. One must therefore believe in the Qur'an, before one can expect any benefit from it.

2. He is required to read it.
Unlike any other book Qur'anic reading, even for Arabs who know the language is in two stages. The first stage is just reading the whole book in small portions from beginning to end and the second stage is reading and understanding it.

3. He is required to understand it.
Qur'anic understanding is graded and gradual understanding. It is not like the restricted understanding of some scientific or mathematical propositions. The first level is ordinary Arabic understanding and meaning of its verses. This understanding can be obtained by reading it in Arabic (for those knowing

the language). Others must read a good translation. The Qur'an has been translated in all languages, but the critical level of understanding can never be achieved from any translation. This is sufficient for many people. The second level of understanding is knowing the Arabic language and reading the Qur'an in Arabic and reading the explanation - *tafsir* - in Arabic or other languages. This is middle understanding. It will ensure a greater understanding of the Qur'an and its message by a person of average education. It is sufficient for most people.

The third level of understanding is in-depth understanding for which an extensive knowledge of classical Arabic, a very broad general education, specialist education in one or more modern science subjects, an intellectual level and curiosity much above the average is a pre-requisite. In-depth understanding of the Qur'an is impossible by anyone who only knows Arabic and is not well versed in other branches of knowledge. This is because many of the verses that explain scientific, astronomical and physical phenomena require some knowledge of these fields to fully understand them.

The highest level of understanding is reserved for persons with above education combined with a high level of *taqwa* and spiritual enlightenment. To them Qur'an is like an ocean in which they can keep sailing and finding new shores even if they were to journey for ever.

4. He is required to act upon its teachings.

This means practice what you have learnt and preach what you practice. Although one feels great delight and joy in reciting or listening to the Qur'an, it is nevertheless not a

---

Tafsir: The commentary on the Qur'an, and its explanation by the learned Muslim/s.
Taqwa: Purity, abstinence, fear of Allah (SWT) piety, righteousness.

book for entertainment. Since its purpose is to guide one on the right path it is essential that one puts its teachings in practice. This putting in practice applies to both the individuals worldly as well as spiritual life within the boundaries of the Qur'anic rules.

5. He is required to convey its message to others.
So that the largest number of persons benefit from its wisdom and teachings each person who has acquired the knowledge of Qur'an must benefit others not only by acting according to its instructions but also by teaching or conveying its message to others. In this way the person who is so taught can derive direct benefit from the Qur'an.

This is based on the advice given in the Qur'an itself in the following verse.

"You are the best people ever sent forth to mankind. You enjoin what is good and forbid what is evil. You believe in Allah... "
(Surah Al-i-Imran 3:110)

It is clear from this brief essay that the depth of wisdom and knowledge hidden in the Qur'an is unlimited. Without its study and without putting its teachings into practice it is impossible for Muslims to succeed in either this world or the Hereafter.

Some selected verses of the Qur'an are given below to whet the reader's appetite for further study. Some of these verses make references to scientific facts that has only been known to man in the last few centuries. At the time the verses were revealed fourteen hundred years ago man did not know these scientific facts. These verses may be of interest to scientists and scholars.

*"Let there be a community among you who will invite
[others] to [do] good, command what is proper and forbid
what is improper; those will be prosperous."*
(Surah Al-i-Imran 3:104)

*"By the declining day, Indeed mankind is in a state of loss,
except those who believe and work good deeds, and
command one another to truth and command one another
to patience and steadfastness."*
(Surah Al-Asr 103:1-3)

*"The (material) things which ye are given are but the
conveniences of this life and the glitter thereof; But that
which is with Allah is better and more enduring: Will ye
not then be wise."*
(Surah Qasas 28:60)

*"... Indeed the noblest among you in the sight of Allah is
the one who is the most righteous of you."*
(Surah Hujuraat 49:13)

*"... Verily never will Allah change the condition of a
people until they change their inner selves ..."*
(Surah Raad 13:11)

*"The parable of those who spend their substance in the
way of Allah is that of a grain of corn; it groweth seven
ears, and each ear hath a hundred grains. Allah giveth
manifold increase to whom he pleaseth: and Allah careth
for all and He knoweth all things."*
(Surah Baqara 2:261)

"And He it is Who has given freedom of movement to the
two great bodies of water-the one sweet and thirst-allaying,
and the other salty and bitter - and yet has wrought
between them a barrier and a forbidding ban. "
(Surah Al-Furqan 25:53)
[This is a reference that the sweet and salt water when rivers
and oceans join do not mix].

"And it is We who have built the universe with (Our
creative) power; and, verily, it is We who are steadily
expanding it. "
(Surah Adh-Dhariyat 51:47)
[This verse clearly foreshadows the modern notion of the
'expanding universe'. It is now a scientific fact that the
cosmos, though finite in extent, is continuously expanding in
space].

"...Allah created thereon two sexes of every (kind) of
plant... "
(Surah Raad 13:3)
[The above verse indicates that there are two sexes to every
kind of plant. A statement fully in accord with botanical
science].

"And the sun: it runs (on its course) withot having any rest
- (and) that is laid down by the will of the Almighty, the
All-Knowing. "
(Surah Ya Seen 36:38)
[This is a reference to the sun moving with its planets
smoothly through space on its path around the galaxy. The
Solar system is made up of nine planets which all move on
almost circular paths, called orbits, around the sun].

There are many verses in the Qur'an confirming universally acclaimed and important scientific facts, some of which have only been discovered by man in the last two hundred years.

The Science and Art of Qur'anic Memorising and Recitation.

An article on Qur'an will be incomplete without a mention of the science of memorising it and the art of reciting it. These are no ordinary accomplishments in Islam that we observe daily but do not perhaps appreciate fully. The first is the science of memorising the Qur'an and the second is the art of reciting it. It is a miracle in itself and is unmatched by any other religion. Millions of Muslims have preserved the Qur'an in their hearts since it was revealed. When one considers each word and each *aya/t* of the Qur'an and the fact that it must be pronounced correctly - there are 6666 *ayat* - that it is only by the blessings of Allah (SWT) and the highly developed science of memorising that both the highly educated and non-educated Muslims are Hafiz-e-Qur'an (those who know Qur'an by heart and can recite it from memory). There is not a single person in the world who has memorised the whole of Bible, the old Testament or the Bhagvad Gita. If this is not a miracle then what is it? The other great achievement is in the area of recitation of Qur'an with *qirah*. To Muslims the beautifully recited verses with *qirah* are music to their ears. It is both inspiring and soul stirring. It is doubtful that any young Muslim would want to hear the Beetles or rock music after hearing the recorded tapes of one of the great *qari's*. The recitation of no other

Qari: Reciter of the Qur'an
Qirah: Melodious chanting of the Qur'an
Aya/t Verse/verses of the Qur'an. Also means signs, proofs, clear evidence or miracles.

book has the same effect on its audience as the Qur'an which can move people to tears even though they may not understand it and to a state of ecstasy those who do. We consider these two above miracles of memorising and reciting the Qur'an a result of Allah's blessings and the genuineness of the book. The great recent advancement in education, knowledge, science and technology has enhanced rather than diminished the appreciation and importance of Qur'an by both less as well as better educated Muslims.

The aya below sums up the universal messsage of the Qur'an.

"But it is nothing less than a message to all the worlds."

(Surah Qalam 68:52)

Hadith

Islam is both a religion and a way of life from birth to death. Guidance to lead a virtuous life is available to Muslims in all areas of human activities - social, cultural, religious, political, financial and moral. The Qur'an lays down the basic laws and in His infinite wisdom Allah (SWT) made possible the detailed rules through the sayings and deeds of Muhammad (SAAS). Muslims now have a complete written code of the basic rules, the detailed rules and also the practical examples of the Prophet (SAAS) to follow. The Arabic word *hadith* means sayings and actions of the Prophet (SAAS) based on authentic reports. *Sunnah* means all the traditions and practices of the Prophet (SAAS) that have become as 'models' to be followed by all Muslims.

Throughout the twenty-three years of Prophet Muhammad's (SAAS) mission his every word and action was noted. These were later compiled by reliable and honourable scholars like *Imam* Bukhari, Muslim, Tirmidhi and others. The sayings of Prophet Muhammad (SAAS) are priceless gems of wisdom and guidance. They are the second most important source of knowledge and guidance after the Qur'an. The following is a selection of the Prophets (SAAS) sayings (*ahadith*) from the books compiled by *Imam* Bukhari and *Imam* Muslim. The accuracy and authenticity of *Imam* Bukhari's book are so great that the religious learned scholars of Islam said concerning his book: 'The most authentic book after the book of Allah (i.e. Al-Qur'an) is Sahih-Al-Bukhari.'

Sunnah: A path, a way, a manner of life. All of the traditions and practices of the Prophet (SAAS), that have become 'models' to be followed by all Muslims.
Sahih Al-Bukhari: The authentic collections of *ahadith* compiled by Imam Bukhari (RA).

◆ The superiority of a learned man over one who only worships is like the superiority of the moon when it is full covering the stars. The learned are heirs of the prophets who do not leave a legacy of dirhams and dinars but only of knowledge. He who acquires knowledge acquires a vast portion.

◆ The search for knowledge is a sacred duty imposed upon every Muslim.

◆ On the day of Judgement, no step of a servant shall move until he has answered covering four things;

1. His body and how he used it.
2. His life and how he spent it.
3. His wealth and how he earned it.
4. His knowledge and what he did with it.

◆ When a person dies, his deeds end except in respect of three matters that he leaves behind;

1. A continuing charity.
2. Knowledge from which benefit could be derived.
3. Righteous offspring who pray for him.

◆ He who has no compassion for our little ones and does not acknowledge the honour due to our elders is not one of us.

◆ Indecency disfigures everything, modesty enhances the charm of everything.

◆ Everyone of you is a steward and is responsible for his charge. A ruler is steward and is accountable for

his domain. A man is a steward of his household. A
wife is a steward of her family.

◆ As you are, so you will have rulers over you.

◆ The most excellent *jihad* is to speak the truth in the
face of a tyrannical ruler.

◆ If anyone walks with an oppressor to strengthen him
knowing that he is an oppressor, he has gone forth
from Islam.

◆ The dearest parts of cities to Allah (SWT) are their
mosques and the most offensive parts are their
markets.

◆ Hasten to do good before you are overtaken by;

Perplexing adversity.
Corrupting prosperity.
Babbling dotage.
Sudden death.

Basic Beliefs and Duties of Muslims

We need to repeat again that Islam is not just a religion but a complete way of life. It has clear Divine rules derived from the Qur'an, supplemented by the Prophet Muhammad's (SAAS) *sunnah* to provide all the guidance man needs to lead a righteous life. Such guidance can only be of real use to those who have faith and are determined to perform the basic duties of Islam.   In Islam, performance of duties without faith and faith without performance of duties is of little use.

It is not possible to have faith without belief.   The Qur'an beautifully sums up belief in the following verses;

"The messenger believes in what has been revealed to him from His Lord, as do the men of faith. Each one (of them) believes in Allah, His angels, His books, and His messengers. "We make no distinction (they say) between one and another of His messengers. And they say: we hear, and we obey: (we seek) Thy forgiveness, our Lord, and to Thee is the End of all journeys. On no soul does Allah place a burden greater than it can bear. It gets every good that it earns, and it is held responsible for anything that it has brought upon itself..."
(Surah Baqara 2: 285-286)

The five basic duties, also known as pillars of Islam are:

Declaration of one's faith	*Shahadah*
The five compulsory daily prayers	*Salah*
The welfare contribution	*Zakah*
The fasting during the month of Ramadan	*Sawm*
The pilgrimage to Makkah	*Hajj*

Shahadah is the declaration of one's belief in the Oneness of Allah (SWT), and the Prophet-hood of Muhammad (SAAS). Without this, one is not a Muslim. It is the foundation pillar of Islam.

Next to *shahadah, salah* is the most important pillar of Islam. All Muslims particularly young Muslims must be reminded that this is one duty, the neglect of which can have far reaching consequences both in this life and the Hereafter. Let us not allow excuses like laziness, TV films, cricket and the like to prevent us from performing *salah. Salah* gives inner strength to one's faith, helps to lead a virtuous life, guarantees personal hygiene and cleanliness, inculcates discipline.

Social security and social welfare systems were introduced in Europe and America only in the last hundred years. Islam introduced a complete Social security system with the compulsory payment of *zakah*, the third pillar of Islam, fourteen hundred years ago. The payment of *zakah* is compulsory on all Muslims who are liable to pay it. *Zakah* rules give details of who is liable to pay and how much he should pay. Taxes paid to the State are not adjustable against the payment of *zakah*.

Fasting in the month of Ramadan is the fourth pillar of Islam. It was prescribed in the following verse of the Holy Qur'an:

"O ye who believe! Fasting is prescribed for you, as it was prescribed for those before you, that ye may ward off (evil)."
(Surah Baqara 2:183)

Fasting has been a part of the universal religious tradition of mankind, though its form and motive vary. Allah (SWT) has ordained fasting for Muslims as a regular exercise of self-discipline and self-purification. They fast from dawn to sunset, for the entire month of Ramadan which is the 9th month of Islamic (lunar) calendar.

Hajj, the 5th pillar of Islam, is the pilgrimage to the 'House of Allah' in Makkah. It is compulsory on every adult Muslim in every part of the world who has the means to undertake the journey.

Hajj is a journey of individual self-renewal for Muslims who are imbued by piety and devotion to Allah (SWT).

It exerts powerful emotions and feelings of universal identity that can be felt when going through the various rites of *hajj* with millions of fellow Muslims from all over the world.

Belief, faith and action are linked in Islam. The purpose of the teachings of the Qur'an and what Allah (SWT) expects from us, human beings, is summed up in the following three verses of Qur'an:

"...Enjoin what is just, and forbid what is wrong..."
(Surah Luqman 31:17)

"Allah commands justice, the doing of good, and helping the relatives. He forbids all shameful deeds, injustice and rebellion..."
(Surah Nahl 16:90)

"...Certainly the noblest among you in the sight of Allah is the most righteous of you..."
(Surah Hujuraat 49:13)

Salah

After *shahadah*, *salah* (five compulsory daily prayers) is the second most important pillar of Islam. *Salah* is the practical proof of a Muslim's faith in Allah (SWT), his belief and devotion to Islam. It has been made compulsory at certain fixed times. Allah (SWT) says in the Qur'an:

".... Salah at fixed times has been enjoined on the believers."
(Surah Nisaa 4:103)

The five daily prayers are *Fajr* (early in the morning), *Zuhr* (early afternoon), *Asr* (late afternoon), *Maghrib* (sunset) and *Isha* (at night before going to bed).

Muslims offer *salah* to remember Allah (SWT) and to be close to Him and gain His favour. This requires abandoning, during the few minutes spent in each *salah,* all material interests in order to provide proof of one's submission and gratitude to Allah (SWT) our Creator.

The Friday congregational prayer (*salatul-Juma*) of early afternoon is conducted at the local mosque or at other suitable gathering place in which the *Imam* of the local mosque or another learned Muslim delivers a sermon before prayer. In addition to the weekly Friday prayer Muslims also have two special annual prayers, one at the end of the month of fasting, *Eid-ul-Fitr* and the other on the occasion of *Eid-ul-Adha* i.e., the time when pilgrimage to Makkah for *Hajj* takes place. Prayers are also held for the Muslim deceased before burial.

'Worship (*ibadah*) is the pillar of religion' is a saying of the Prophet Muhammad (SAAS). The Qur'an speaks of

---

Imam: A responsible, knowledgeable Muslim leader. The person who leads the others in a prayer.

worship more than a hundred times and calls it variously as *salah* (prayer for Allah), *dua* (appeal to Allah), *dhikr* (remembering Allah), *tasbih* (glorifying of Allah) and *inabah* (returning or attaching to Allah).

Ablution or ritual washing and being physically clean is a pre-requisite before the service of worship. In this ritual purification one has to wash the hands, the mouth, the nose, the face, the arms, the head, the ears and the feet. Washing them is not merely the outward cleanliness; it is also repentance for the past and resolution for the future.

The preferable and more formal way of worship is the congregational service at the local community mosque. In the absence of such possibility or lacking adequate alternate facility one prays alone and individually man or woman or with members of one's family. In schools, colleges, universities and at work Muslims must make every effort for congregational prayers and if this is not possible then they must find a clean quiet corner to offer their *Zuhr* and *Asr* prayers and other prayers if applicable. It is important to pray properly and correctly and those who have any doubts on any aspect of prayer must seek the guidance of other knowledgeable Muslims or benefit from many excellent publications giving full details regarding the ritual of *salah* and other related matters.

Salah has many beneficial effects on its performers. The first is military like discipline and self control that are acquired. It also encourages high standards of cleanliness; safeguards against both minor and major sins; brings us in contact with fellow Muslims (through congregational prayers) in the community. The spiritual benefits will be in direct proportion to the devotion, concentration and humility with which *salah* is offered. One feels transported to the presence of Allah (SWT) and feels the blessings and *Nur* of the Creator. This feeling is beyond the power of human beings to describe. Without material, idol-like, symbols, the believer travels, towards the transcendent Allah (SWT), on a spiritual journey. Furthermore the faithful in all parts of the globe, turn their faces, during the service of worship, towards the same focal point, the *Kaba* - the House of Allah in Makkah. This reminds them of the unity of the world Community of Muslims, without distinction of class, race, colour or region.

No other religion in the world has comparable prayer like *salah* of Islam. *Salah* has its unique simplicity and plainness without any material or noisy paraphernalia. Yet it exerts powerful emotions. The recitation of the Qur'an particularly during the night and early morning prayers, when it is so quiet and still, quickly transports one to ultimate peace and contentment even in these traumatic and noisy times. A person who prays thus never needs the stimulation of drugs or alcohol to forget it all!

Prayer without faith is meaningless. It is like travelling without a ticket with no destination in mind. The Qur'an confirms this in the following verse.

"For Him (alone) is prayer in Truth: any others they call upon besides Him hear them no more than if they were to stretch forth their hands for water to reach their mouths but it reaches them not: for the prayer of those without Faith is nothing but (futile) wandering (in the mind)."
(Surah Raad 13:14)

Nur: Light. Also the title of the 24th Surah of the Qur'an.
An-Nur: One of the attributes of Allah (SWT).

Zakah

Welfare and Social security systems in many countries are a modern phenomena. The Social security system in UK was established after the last great war. Before this the poor and the needy of these islands depended on alms houses and the charity of individuals or church/salvation army soup kitchens.

It must therefore come as a surprise to non-Muslims that the Islamic welfare system was established by Divine Commandment fourteen hundred years ago and was fully functional soon after the Prophet's death.

The means used to establish this was through *zakah,* an Arabic word used in the Qur'an. It has comprehensive meaning with no equivalent word in the English language. The word *zakah* has a broad conceptual meaning incorporating charity, alms, official tax, kindness, purification etc. It is not a tax that by some clever planning one can avoid to pay, nor it is a voluntary contribution to some cause where one has discretion whether to pay or not to pay. It is a religious duty enjoined by Allah (SWT) that must be discharged by Muslims of certain means for the welfare of and in the interest of society as a whole. Purity is the literal meaning of *zakah* while the technical meaning of the word for our purpose is welfare contribution of an annual amount in money or goods by Muslims which must be distributed to the rightful beneficiaries. Rules of *zakah* define and clarify the list of rightful beneficiaries.

After *shahadah* and *salah, zakah* is the third most important pillar of Islam. It is an exceptionally remarkable Muslim institution.

Rate and collection of Zakah.

Zakah is payable if total value of net assets which one holds for a full lunar year exceeds *nisab*. At present the *nisab* in UK is approximately £700.00 (or about US $1100.00). This is based on the value of 3oz of gold or 21oz of silver. The *nisab* amount may vary from year to year depending on the market value of these metals. An example will illustrate what *nisab* means. When you pay income tax you normally deduct the allowances and pay the tax at the specified rates on the balance. In the case of *nisab* however, *zakah* is payable on the whole net amount if it exceeds *nisab* value (currently £700.00). Thus *nisab* determines those who are exempt from the obligations of *zakah* - all those whose net wealth is currently less than £700.00.

The chief category of assets on which *zakah* is payable are listed below.

Assets   £

Cash at home
Balance in bank account
Gold and silver including jewellery
Stocks and shares at current market value
Stock in trade and business
Equity in property held as investment

Total gross value of zakahtable assets   ....
Less immediate debts   ....

Zakahtable total   £ ***

If the zakahtable total exceeds £700.00 then *zakah* is payable at the rate of 2.5% on the whole of this amount.

Notes.

a. The capital of a business including working capital is zakahtable. The average net value over 12 months may be taken for this calculation. *Zakah* on profit earned in the business in the current year is payable the next year.

Nisab: Property or estate on which zakah must be paid at the rate of two and half percent of its net value.

b. Vehicles, equipment, fixtures and fittings used in the business are not zakahtable.

c. *Zakah* cannot be adjusted against income or poll tax or any other tax paid to state or local authorities.

d. Overdrafts, debts (both credit card and other consumer credit debts and money borrowed from friends and relatives) are deductible. Mortgage on the security of the house repayable over a number of years is not deductible.

If you have any doubts in working out the amount of *zakah* payable then please contact one of the larger Muslim organisations such as mentioned here or your local *Imam*.

Who should the Zakah be paid to?

Zakah may be distributed directly to needy individuals or to established Muslim welfare organisations set up for this purpose. In the United Kingdom *zakah* can be paid to Muslim Aid, Muslim Relief, Bait al-Mal al-Islami, all of whom are well respected and well established institutions. An issue may need clarification here. Europe and America now have comprehensive social security systems to take care of the basic needs of its citizens/residents including Muslims, who are entitled to benefits according to the rules. A suitable use of *zakah* funds in these countries would be for the education and small business development of Muslims. Scholarships can be granted to bright but poor Muslims for higher studies and research and for the tuition of school students to improve their chances of university entrance. Perhaps a better use of these funds may be in the area of reducing unemployment among the Muslims particularly young Muslims. A small capital grant with some management assistance may enable many Muslims to set up small self-employed service, repair, manufacturing and consulting businesses. They in turn would help the local community, reduce national employment and generally become better and more productive members of society.

Wisdom of Zakah.

1. Since it is a Divine order *zakah* is deemed to purify the property of the *zakah* payer and help him avoid greed and selfishness.

2. *Zakah* alleviates the suffering of the needy and helpless members of society.

3. Islam encourages enterprise, wealth creation and wealth generation. A Muslim who makes money by legitimate means and pays *zakah* feels truly contented.

4. It is an insurance against social unrest and jealousy. If poorer members of the community are being looked after they are not likely to be jealous of their richer brothers particularly in a society where equal opportunity exists for all.

5. *Zakah* promotes social and community consciousness in the Muslims and is a great character building institution.

6. The richer a Muslim society the lesser the need for *zakah*. The collected *zakah* funds will then be deposited in the state treasury and could become substantial sums. Part of these funds could be used for the advancement of education, useful research and other productive activities that directly benefit the Muslim community. Some of the funds can also be used for the benefit of those outside one's own country.

No welfare or social security system has yet been developed that surpasses the simplicity and effectiveness of this Islamic welfare system.

The Qur'an says :

"The Believers, men and women, are protectors, one of another: they enjoin what is just, and forbid what is evil: they observe regular prayers, practise regular charity (zakah), and obey Allah and His Apostle. On them Allah will pour His mercy: for Allah is Exalted in power, Wise."
(Surah Tauba 9:71)

Sawm

Abstention from food is considered a fast in normal terms. Consequently going without food or without food and water is fasting. Many non-Muslims practice some form of fasting. They do so for different reasons - physical, mental, spiritual or political. The Hindus consider fasting a meritorious act and they fast on many special occasions. The Jews fast on the 10th day (Yom Kippor) of the month of Tishri. They fast for atonement following the injunction laid down in the Torah. Christians fast in Lent according to the Bible. They fast in penitence and in commemoration of the birth of Jesus (AS). But none of the above fasts are genuine fasts. In all these fasts some form of food or liquid can be taken. Also they do not fully combine the three ingredients of fast, that is, physical, mental and spiritual such as that practised in the Islamic month of fasting, i.e. *Ramadan.* Islamic fasting is total abstention from food and drink from dawn to dusk. And this is just one element of Islamic fasting. The greater element of Islamic fasting is devotion and worship, charity and caring, personal self development and Allah (SWT) consciousness - *taqwa* - and avoidance of all forms of sinful and unsocial acts. All this is expected to be accomplished while the Muslim is going about his normal duties of earning a living or attending to the daily chores. The only exception being the last ten days of fasting when any Muslim wishing to do so may retire to the local mosque for concentrated devotion and prayer. But this requirement is not obligatory.

Islam has institutionalised fasting as a regular exercise in self discipline and self purification. The Qur'an, following the previous revelations, reaffirms the continuity of fasting as

---

Taqwa: Purity, abstinence, fear of Allah (SWT), piety, righteousness.

an obligatory duty of Muslims. Muslims fast from dawn to dusk for the entire month of Ramadan, the 9th month of the Islamic lunar calendar.

Fasting - *sawm or siyam* - is one of the five pillars of Islam. The Prophet Muhammad (SAAS) is reported to have said:

'The superstructure of Islam is raised on five pillars: Tawhid - the Oneness of Allah (SWT), Salah - the establishment of Prayers, Zakah - the payment of poor due, Sawm - the fast of Ramadan and Hajj - the pilgrimage to Makkah.'
(Bukhari and Muslim)

Fasting has been made obligatory by the following verse of the Qur'an:

"O ye who believe! Fasting is prescribed for you, even as it was prescribed for those before you, that ye may ward off (evil)."
(Surah Baqara 2:183)

Allah (SWT) revealed the Qur'an, the greatest book of guidance in the month of Ramadan. It is a very blessed month as it contains a night, *Lailatul-Qadr* which is better than a thousand months. It is a month whose beginning is mercy, whose middle is forgiveness and whose end is freedom from hell.

Fasting commences with a light pre-dawn meal called *suhur* and with *niyah* or intention of fast. Fasting ends with *iftar* which means breaking the fast after sunset. *Iftar* is eaten after making the following *dua* for breaking the fast.

Dua: Supplication, prayer, invocation to Allah (SWT).
Lailatul-Qadr: The night of power. A mysterious and blessed night during the month of Ramadan.

'O Allah! I fasted for Your sake, and I am breaking my fast from the sustenance you have blessed me with, accept it from me.'

The institution of fasting influences a Muslim society in a positive way. Fasting enhances the feeling of inner peace and provides tranquillity of mind. It teaches patience and perseverance. It is also the best programme to cut down over indulgence and to give the digestive system some rest. In addition, an attitude of sharing, concern, caring, humility is instilled in those who fast. Fasting develops *taqwa* - Allah consciousness which develops piety. In Islam the most pious are the most beloved and most honoured in the sight of Allah (SWT). During this month millions of Muslims all over the world ask for forgiveness of their sins and exert themselves in prayer, invocation and in reciting Allah's (SWT) book. A special reading of the Qur'an is completed through *tarawih* prayer which is performed in congregation after the *isha* prayers.

Fasting in Islam is not done as a penance. It is undertaken for the pleasure and for the sake of Allah (SWT) for which there is a mighty reward in the Hereafter.

The feast of fast breaking at the end of the month is marked by the festivities of *Eid-ul-fitr*. It begins with a special congregational prayer and thanksgiving followed by rejoicing among family, friends and neighbours. *Zakatul-fitr* is payable before the *Eid* prayers. It is preferable to pay it a few days before so that the poor and needy members of the community can also make arrangements for *Eid* and take part in its festivities.

Like *hajj* the institution of fasting unifies Muslim societies and regulates their social lives. All Muslims, male and female, rich and poor go through the same experience of fasting with no special privileges or favours to anyone. This practice simultaneously followed by all the Muslims in the world every year for the entire month of Ramadan establishes equality, unity and contributes towards a more virtuous and strong *Ummah*. Fasting is based on the Muslim lunar calendar. Thus, each year Ramadan falls on a different date and different part of the season. Over a period of approximately 33 years fasting in any country will have been experienced in all seasons; summer, autumn, winter and spring. This is unique as no one community in the Muslim world, because of its location in a certain time and temperature zone, can permanently face fasting in the same season. They will experience fasting in all seasons and at all times of the year possibly up to three times if they are blessed with a long life. The same, of course, applies to the Islamic festivals.

Hajj and Umrah

Hajj is the pilgrimage to the 'House of Allah' in Makkah. It is compulsory on every adult Muslim in any part of the world who has the means to undertake the journey. *Hajj* is the fifth pillar of Islam. Every year it brings together what may justly be described as the largest gathering of mankind. Thus *hajj* is a very special annual event, unlike anything that any other religion has in the world. For fourteen hundred years Muslims have been gathering annually in *Makkah* without interruption in response to their Lord's Commandment in order to express their devotion to Him.

Hajj is, above all, a journey of individual self-renewal inspired by piety and devotion to Allah (SWT). In this quest, the individual is strengthened by the knowledge that thousands of human beings from all over the world regardless of their worldly status, language or race, are in pursuit of the same objective- the pleasure of their Creator.

Many of the rites of the *hajj* date from the days of Prophet *Ibrahim* (AS). There is a sense of history, in going along the same straight path that has been the way of the prophets of Allah (SWT) in the past and those who followed them. There is also a natural feeling of universal and brotherly identity among the pilgrims as they go anti-clockwise around the cube-like building of the *Kaba,* clothed in the simple garments of the state of *ihraam,* or as they stand deeply inspired on the plain of *Arafat* from noon until sunset.

The powerful emotions experienced during this act of worship and international gathering are difficult to describe

---

Kaba: The cube. A cube like building built by Ibrahim (AS) and his son Ismail (AS) in the centre of the great mosque in Makkah towards which all Muslims turn their face in prayer.
Ihraam: A state in which one is prohibited to practice certain deeds that are lawful at other times. The ceremonies of *hajj* and *umrah* are performed in such a state.

as they are so personal to each pilgrim.

Hajj, unlike any other occasion, has the capacity to lay bare the fancies and vanities of man. The *talbiyya* or the special refrain announcing man's willingness and eagerness to acknowledge and obey Allah (SWT) resounds throughout the *Hajj* environment:

'LABBAIK ALLAHUMMA LABBAIK
LABBAIK LA SHARIKA LA KA LABBAIK.
MINAL HAMDAH WA NEMATAKA WAL MUSLAKA LA
SHARIKA LAKA.'
'Here I am, O Lord, here I am!
Here I am; no partner hast Thou; here I am!
Surely to Thee is all Praise, all goodness and all
Sovereignty; No partner hast Thou!'

The simplicity, beauty and power of this humble but poignant refrain creates the mood in which the pilgrimage is performed. It is important that the very highest standard of conduct and excellence of manner is displayed by each pilgrim. Arrangements and facilities for *hajj* have improved a great deal in recent years but at the same time intrusion by too much technology affects the sombre mood of *hajj.* It is essential to maintain a happy balance. As far as possible natural solutions to ecological and environmental problems due to such a large gathering of humans, should be found. This would ensure the spirit and the atmosphere of contemplation, devotion and personal rectification that are the prime objectives of this pilgrimage.

The Qur'an gives guidance on the code of conduct to be adopted at *hajj* in the following verse.

"For Hajj are the months well known. Whoever
undertakes the pilgrimage shall, while on pilgrimage,

Talbiyya: Waiting or standing for orders. Saying, *Labbaik, Allahumma Labbaik* loudly from the beginning to the end of *hajj* or *umrah,* meaning that I am present to respond to your call O' Allah.

abstain from lewd speech, from all wicked conduct, and from quarrelling; and whatever good you may do, Allah is aware of it. And make provision for yourselves-but, verily, the best of all provisions is Allah-consciousness: remain then conscious of Me, O you who are endowed with insight."
(Surah Baqara 2:197)

It is therefore essential that steps are taken to ensure that the mood of *hajj* is not marred or ruined by the environment and the physical conditions under which *hajj* is performed. The prior briefing and education of pilgrims in the ritual and courtesies of *hajj* would be useful.

The following is a brief summary of the rituals of *hajj*:

a. Changing to '*Ihraam*', prior to arriving in Makkah.

b. Arrival in Makkah and going around the *Kaba*. This is called *Tawaf.*

c. Hastening between the two hills called *Safa* and *Marwah*. This is called *Sa'y.*

d. Halting at Mount *Arafat* on the 9th of the month of *Dhu Al-Hijjah.*

e. Staying overnight at *Muzdalifa.*

f. Staying at *Mina.*

g. Stoning at *Jamarat-ul-Aqaba.*

h. *Tawaf.*

j. The sacrifice offering at *Mina.*

Although not part of the *hajj* ritual many pilgrims on *hajj* visit the Prophet's (SAAS) mosque at Madinah where he is buried. The Prophet's (SAAS) mosque is the second holiest place in Islam. This is highly recommended because by visiting Madinah one is paying his respects to the greatest teacher of mankind ever born and whose life continues to be a source of guidance and inspiration to millions.

Umrah, a minor form of *hajj* can be performed any time of the year. Except for *Tawaf* and *Sa'y* and of course the prayer in *Masjid-al-Haram* other rituals of *hajj* are not obligatory for *umrah*.

Duties of Parents to their Children

In Islam, parents have the obligation to cherish, sustain, educate and train their children. This obligation begins even before the children are born. Take the institution of marriage. Before a Muslim couple marry each other they must look for the quality of *taqwa* and righteousness in each other. The choice of a spouse by wealth, beauty, professional qualifications and lineage is not important in Islam. It is *taqwa* and righteousness. Righteousness and *taqwa*, according to the Prophet (SAAS), are the most important qualities in a Muslim. Thus parents responsibilities begin with each partner's beliefs, attitudes and good conduct in a marriage. A couple are advised by the Prophet (SAAS) to pray for children who are *saalih* - noble and righteous.

A mother in particular should ensure that she lives an Islamic life style because her physical and psychological state may affect the unborn child.

Once the child is born and until he or she is under age two, a mother has great responsibility for the rearing, comforting and upbringing of the child.

It is a sad reflection on the present Western civilisation that it gives preference and accords a higher status to sales girls, models, actresses, secretaries, business executives and business women compared to that of the mother. The breakdown in discipline and the increase in children's crime is a direct result of this attitude.

As the children start growing up greater responsibility passes on to the father in the *tarbiyyah* of the child. *Tarbiyyah* implies not only looking after, nourishing and helping the child to grow but also to take care of his/her

Tarbiyyah: Education, training, nurturing, looking after children, particularly inculcating good manners in them.

emotional and psychological needs. A parent must strive to inspire confidence in the children, promote creativity and innovation, establish mutual trust when need be. They must also be firm in not allowing un-Islamic behaviour by their children.

After parents the responsibility for the education and upbringing of a Muslim child rests on grandparents, uncles, aunts, sisters, brothers and Muslim neighbours and teachers. They all have an important and responsible role to play in the education and upbringing of a Muslim child. Parents who expect their children to be disciplined and to work hard must be disciplined and work hard themselves. Parents should ensure that their children are happy and cheerful and have a zest for life and living. The children must experience the carefree joy and excitement of growing up. They should be trained to grow up with the attitude, habits and etiquettes of Islam. The virtues and habits that they should develop are:
- **honesty and truthfulness.**
- **attitude of helpfulness and being considerate.**
- **cleanliness and tidiness.**

They need to develop the manners and etiquettes of Islam such as when and how to greet, how to speak, sit, eat, how to be reverent in *salah*, attentive in class, robust and full of zest in play.

Their physical fitness is also essential. It is of paramount importance for Muslim children to be physically fit, strong and courageous. They must learn as many sports as they can and should take active interest in games and physical fitness activities. Parents should encourage their children to take part in Muslim group activities, youth camps, group social work, lectures and seminars particularly during school and college holidays. This should be done from an early age. Active involvement in a Young Muslim or Muslimah group or the college and university Islamic society is a must for every young Muslim. They must also maintain good and harmonious relations with non-Muslims at school, college, work place or neighbourhood and must show kindness and consideration towards the elderly, the sick and the children. It is the duty of parents to instill these qualities in their children.

It is also important for children to develop a thirst for knowledge. The first and most important knowledge for a Muslim child is the ability to recite the Qur'an preferably with full understanding of its meaning. He must then study as much as possible *hadith, seerah* and other books on Islam.

Both the Qur'an and the Prophet (SAAS) encourage Muslims to acquire as much knowledge and education as possible. This desire and ambition to acquire knowledge must be instilled by parents in their children early in life, and where necessary the parents should make the necessary sacrifices for it. Non Arabic speaking Muslims wishing to learn the language to enable them to read and understand the Qur'an should start early. It is difficult to recommend a starting age as circumstances may vary for each child. But it should be borne in mind that as they reach eleven they are expected to learn an additional language at their schools in Europe and America and this may not be Arabic.

A Muslim child must be given the best possible education and skill training in line with his abilities. This is essential in the present competitive society to enable him to compete on equal terms. Education also helps one to become a better member of society, and enables him in conjunction with proper training to earn a lawful livelihood and be of service to fellow Muslims in particular and to all human beings in general.

The care of every Muslim child, particularly those without parents becomes the responsibility of the entire Muslim community. References to children/child in this article mean both female and male children with no distinction whatsoever. Girls must be given the same equal opportunity in education as the boys.

Children's Duties to Parents

Children's duties towards parents has been fully explained both by Divine injunctions in the Qur'an and the Prophet's *sunnah*   The relationship of the Muslim to his parents has the highest priority over all others except Allah (SWT) and His Prophet (SAAS). This relationship includes financial, emotional and spiritual responsibilities towards his or her parents and is on an on-going basis even after the death of one's parents.

The reward for satisfactory discharge of this duty towards parents is paradise. Failure to discharge this duty will render a Muslim to Allah's (SWT) displeasure and His punishment.

In general all obligations of responsibility to parents include both father and mother. It should be noted that children have a greater degree of responsibility towards mother in Islam. A man came to Allah's Prophet (SAAS) and said, "O Prophet of Allah! 'Who is more entitled to be treated with the best companionship by me?' The Prophet (SAAS) said, 'your mother'. The man said, 'then who?' The Prophet (SAAS) said, 'your mother'. The man further said, 'then who?' The Prophet (SAAS) said, 'your mother'. The man asked again 'then who?' The Prophet (SAAS) said 'then your father'." (Bukhari and Muslim)

There are many verses in the Qur'an, which command the believers for the good treatment of parents. The two are:

"...worship non save Allah (only), and be good to parents..."
(Surah Baqara 2:83)

"...And do good (show kindness) unto parents, and unto kinsfolk and orphans, and the needy..."
(Surah Nisaa 4:36)

How important Muslim parents are is clear from the saying that their rights are next to those of Almighty Allah (SWT) in Islam? Another saying that heaven is under the feet of mother confirms the importance of this responsibility.

When parents become old, their temperament may change. They can become easily irritable and short-tempered due to their age and frailty. Their children should take these changes of temperament for granted and show considerable patience and magnanimity for their ageing parents.

The children should adopt attitudes of humbleness, politeness and obedience towards parents. They should recall those days of infancy when they were totally dependent on their parents.

According to Islam it is compulsory for every Muslim to show goodness and mercy and to act righteously towards his parents throughout their lives. It applies even to parents who are non-Muslims. This shows great generosity and tolerance of Islam. These rights of parents cannot take precedence over the rights of Allah (SWT). Allah (SWT) commands disobedience to those parents who promote *shirk* or ask their children to associate anything or anyone else with Allah (SWT) or who ask their children to commit any act which involves disobedience to Allah (SWT).

Muslims find it distressing that so many older parents are treated badly in Western society. In many families older parents are considered a burden. Such parents often end up in old people's homes and lead a life without the companionship and affection of their own children and grand children. No believing Muslim is likely to neglect his parents as such. To say that older people cannot live with younger generation of their children or grand children is nonsense. Millions of Muslims all over the world including Europe and America seem to be managing quite well.

Shirk: Polytheism, idolatry, paganism, to worship others along with Allah (SWT).

Islam and the Acquisition of Knowledge

Knowledge is a unique gift of the Creator to man. Knowledge is vital for success in this world and the Hereafter. It is the basis of man's progress in this world and a vital factor in his well-being after death. It is knowledge that has made man superior to every other Creation of Allah (SWT). When Allah (SWT) created man he equipped him with a wealth of knowledge.

The very first revelation to Muhammad (SAAS) from Allah (SWT) begins with reference to knowledge. The verses are quoted below:

"Proclaim! (or Read) in the name of thy Lord and Cherisher, Who created.... He Who taught (the use of) the Pen, taught man that which he knew not."
(Surah Alaq 96:1,5)

Here the words read, teach, pen have been used by Allah (SWT). They are significant elements in the search for knowledge. The root words in Arabic for teach, read, pen have far broader meanings and harmony and cannot be translated in the English to retain and convey the depth of meaning of the Arabic text. They imply reading, writing, books, study, investigation, research including science, self knowledge, and spiritual understanding.

Importance of acquiring knowledge is further emphasised in the Qur'an by the well known Qur'anic prayer:

"...my Lord! Advance me in knowledge."
(Surah Ta-Ha 20:114)

The first obligation on every Muslim is acquisition of knowledge. Correct knowledge precedes correct action. How a Muslim acquires correct knowledge and how he uses it is also important. This determines whether he is fulfilling his role in the world according to Allah's Commandments. It is therefore important for a Muslim to acquire the right type of knowledge by searching for accurate sources and by applying proper ways in its acquisition. The Muslim should then use the knowledge so acquired in a *halal*, useful and constructive way.

Some Muslims think that the acquisition of worldly knowledge of Science, Engineering, Medicine etc. is not important. They feel that Muslims should devote most of their time acquiring the knowledge of Qur'an, *hadith* and related matters. This assumption is incorrect and has no authority for it in the Qur'an and *sunnah*. No restrictions have been placed on Muslims in the acquisition of useful and true knowledge. Indeed, there are exhortations and pointers in the Qur'an to acquire as much knowledge as possible.

Numerous authentic *hadith* are also related to the Prophet (SAAS) on the importance of acquiring knowledge. The following are a selection from Bukhari and Muslim:

'To seek knowledge is a sacred duty of every Muslim, male or female.'

'He who acquires knowledge acquires a vast portion.'

'If anyone goes on his way in search of knowledge, Allah (SWT) will thereby, make easy for him the way to Paradise.'

The acquisition of Islamic knowledge must be given highest priority. This means that every Muslim must acquire the knowledge of the Creator and knowledge of man and his functioning that will bring him closer to the Creator. The Muslim must then acquire the knowledge of what is right and wrong, lawful and unlawful. This must be followed by the knowledge of the role of prophets and in particular of the last Prophet (SAAS), his life and work. Thus equipped he is free to acquire knowledge of nature in its broadest sense - physical sciences, the use of reason, observation and experimentation, astronomy, mathematics, engineering, agriculture, physics and chemistry, biology, oceanography, manufacturing, languages or any other branch of knowledge or profession except those that are manifestly unlawful.

The first type of knowledge is acquired through the study of Qur'an, *hadith, seerah* and other Islamic publications such as books, magazines, research papers and activities such as seminars and lectures. The basic source of this first knowledge, however, remain the three - Qur'an, *hadith* and *seerah*. The second type of knowledge is acquired through what some people wrongly term as secular education or Western education, which they are not, since no one has monopoly on knowledge. Reference to knowledge in Islam means the total knowledge made up of the above two parts. It is of course true that some Muslims having acquired the first part of this knowledge may wish to proceed with the second part to become scientists, surgeons, astronomers etc. There will be others who may wish to go further and deeper in acquiring the first part of the knowledge by specialising in *fiqh*, Islamic banking, *shari'ah* to become the learned scholars of Islam.

In future many gifted Muslims should endeavour to

Seerah: Study of the life of Muhammad (SAAS).
Fiqh: Islamic jurisprudence specially used in regard to law and its applications.
Shari'ah: Islamic law based on the Qur'an, *hadith, Ijma* and *Qiyas*. (See article on Islamic State/Political System for further explanation).

acquire both general/scientific knowledge at advanced level combined with the equally advanced level of knowledge of Qur'an, *hadith* and the Arabic language. Such Muslims would be better placed to serve Islam.

It needs to be clarified that the acquisition of degrees or professional qualifications are means to the end, not the end itself. The end is continuous exertion in the pursuit and application of knowledge and skills.

The responsibility rests on Muslim parents, community teachers, community and religious leaders to emphasise the importance of education and acquisition of knowledge to all members of the community. It finally rests with our young Muslims and Muslimahs. All Muslims should realise that no sacrifice is too great in the pursuit of this objective. This is one occupation from which there is no retirement. One learns until one dies. The acquisition of knowledge and wisdom and its use in the service of Allah (SWT) and His creation is a continuing process all through one's life. These are not just fancy statements but declaration of fact.

In Islam the purpose in acquiring knowledge is not only to be able to earn a lawful living but also to use it for the benefit of mankind, to eradicate suffering and poverty, to educate others, to learn to distinguish between right and wrong and to serve the Creator and His creation in whatever capacity one can.

The flow chart showing the recommended route in acquiring knowledge may prove useful to readers.

FLOW CHART OF
RECOMMENDED ROUTE
FOR THE EDUCATION OF
MUSLIMS/MUSLIMAHS

Reading and under-
standing of Qur'an,
Hadith and Sunnah.
Learning of Arabic
language.

Basic General
Education

*1. Basic compulsory
Level of knowledge*

Further studies of
Qur'an Hadith
Seerah

Further Education at
college and university up
to and including degree
level

*2. Medium Level
of Knowledge*

Other books on Islam, Muslims
and learning of advanced
Arabic language

Specialist advanced
level education at
post-graduate level
for those Muslims who
wish to delve deep in
the religious
knowledge

Continuing On-going
education in Qur'an,
Hadith and current
affairs concerning Islam

Advanced education
in the professions or
at post-graduate and
research level.

*3. Advanced level
of knowledge*

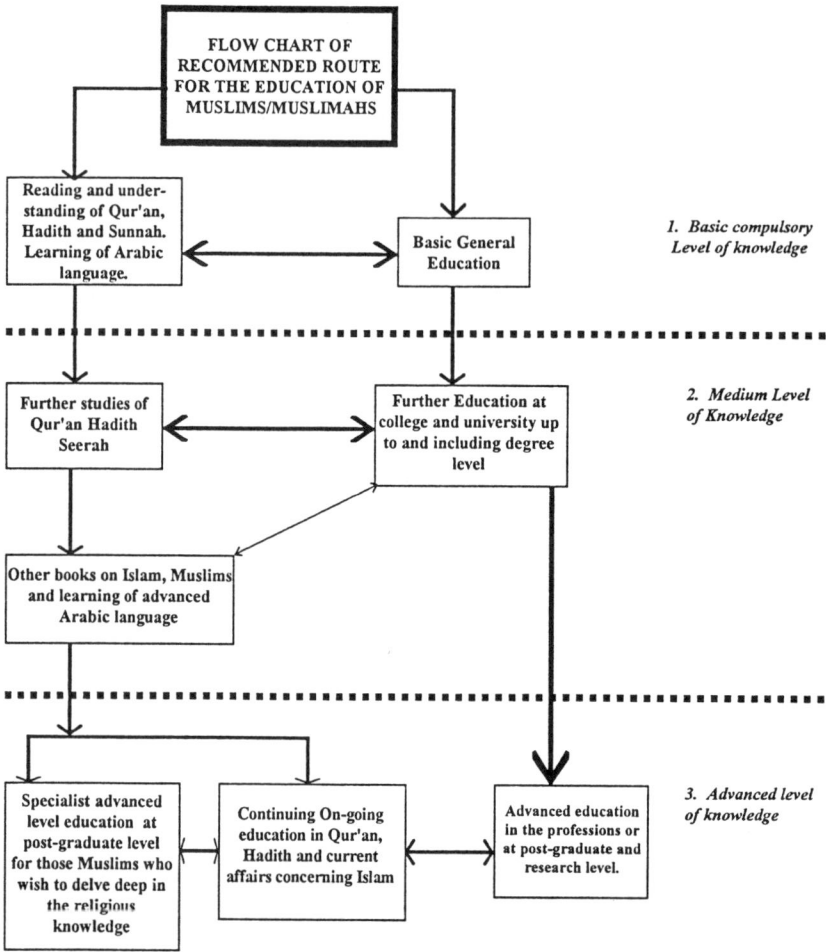

"To seek knowledge is a sacred duty of every Muslim, male or female". (Bukhari and Muslim)

The Mosque in Islam

Introduction.

Whenever and wherever in their long history, Muslims neglected the basic teachings and practices of Qur'an and *sunnah* either because of ignorance, carelessness or evolving fashion they were pounced, trounced and denounced by others. There are two contributory factors that brought about such neglect. The first was integration and identification with Western values and culture on the assumption that West meant 'good'. The second is misuse or lack of use of one or more of their institutions. Or perhaps not knowing how to make effective use of an existing institution. Both factors above have directly contributed to Muslim's present day decline. In this article we deal with the latter.

The most important Muslim institution, the mosque, is a glaring example of such neglect. Muslims are also reminded how urgent it is for them to revive this institution and to put it to the full use for which it was intended.

The Mosque as a Building Structure.

A mosque is a Muslim place of worship. The name mosque means a place for prostration. The Arabic word *masjid* means any house or open space for prayer. *Jami masjid* or 'collective mosque' is the centre of community worship. In the early days of Islam a city might have many mosques but only one collective mosque or *jami masjid* where the Friday prayers were performed.

The first mosques were modelled on the place of worship of the Prophet Muhammad (SAAS) - the courtyard of his house at Madinah - and these were plots of ground marked as sacred, and partly roofed.

The feature of a typical mosque is described below:

Courtyard.
It precedes the prayer hall to accommodate the overflow of worshippers.

Ablution Area.
Fountains or other forms of water supply to wash before prayer. Can be inside the mosque or in the courtyard.

The Minaret.
A tower structure to call the believers to prayer. Often the call to prayer is now made using the loud speaker. In Islamic countries this call by loudspeaker is sometimes synchronised and produces a beautiful sound particularly during morning and night prayer calls. Sadly such calls may not be heard in Western countries as many cities do not allow it.

The Mihrab.
It is a semicircular niche reserved for the prayer leader-*Imam* - and points to the *qibla* - the direction of Makkah.

The Minbar.
This consists of steps, sometimes enclosed by hand rails, leading to a seat or platform and often covered by a canopy. It is from this *minbar* that the Friday sermon - *khutba* - is delivered by the preacher *khatib* or *Imam* or some other Muslim.

Riwaq.
In larger mosques the courtyard is often surrounded by an arcade called in Arabic - *riwaq*. It also provides residential accommodation to students who study at the *madrasah* associated with the mosque.

There are mosques in Middle East, India and Pakistan that are among some of the finest buildings in the world. The recently built king Hassan mosque in Casablanca, Morocco is an engineering wonder. One feels awed by its power, majesty and glory. For centuries Muslim architects have designed superb places of worship. There are no paintings or statues in a mosque. The walls are decorated with abstract Islamic design - mosaics and verses from the Qur'an written in beautiful calligraphy. The feeling inside a mosque is one of solitude, contemplation, majesty in simplicity, reverence and humility to the Creator.

The Mosque as an Institution.

Muslims do not have Western type of institutions like pubs and clubs. The mosque has always been a central institution for Muslims, since the time of the Prophet (SAAS). It has been the centre of Muslim's social, educational, religious and political activities. While the primary purpose of the mosque as the House of Allah (SWT) is as a place of worship, it has always been the focal point of the Muslim community. It is used for the religious education and instruction of the young, and as a centre for social and cultural activities for men and women of the local community wherever the *Imam* and the mosque committees are enlightened and the local community is far-sighted. In the past mosques have also been used as medical centres, a place for the distribution of *zakah*, for special military functions and as centres for dealing with any crisis facing the community.

Sadly, this role of the mosque has been allowed to run down to our bitter disadvantage and with far reaching consequences. In many countries but particularly in Europe and America Muslims have built thousands of mosques over the past 50 years. If there is a sizeable community of Muslims in any town or city in Europe or America then there is a mosque. Muslims have also formed a plethora of organisations for the benefit of the community. No doubt this has been done with the best of intentions. However, neither the mosques nor these organisations have made much impact on the community and the neighbourhood at grassroots level.

Presently some mosques have become one or more of the following:

- A political battlefield for some power hungry members of the committee.

- A centre of religious and sectarian clique and conflict supported by some powerful group or even a foreign government.

- A depository for the appointment and retention of *Imams* with little or no knowledge of local language; no higher general education and in some cases no knowledge of the Arabic language.

- An institution that bans local Muslim women and Muslim children from holding any social, cultural or *dars* activities.

An Islamic institution as old as Islam itself which is supposed to be the nerve centre of the community has become in some cases only its lifeless symbol. There are, of course, exceptions represented by some active mosques with excellent management and very fine *Imams* - well versed both in religious and secular education and with good

---

Dars: Religious discourse, lesson or teaching.
Imam: Responsible knowledgeable leader. The person who leads Muslims in a prayer.
Ummah: A nation, a people, a sect. Usually refers to Muslim community.

command of both the local language and Arabic. But they are in a minority.

Islamic revival on a global scale is now making its impact felt. Inspired by a desire to contribute Muslims have set up many organisations for this purpose both locally and internationally. The *Ummah* is being made aware of this through the media. However, there is presently no institution or organisation, on an international scale, which can claim to have the size and the resources to do grassroots work on such a large scale towards this revival. The efforts of many organisations have been fragmented producing minimal results not because Muslims lack the capacity for hard work or are unwilling to take up the challenge. They lack management and organisational skills, they have little training in logistics and strategy and are often incapable in combining clear objectives with executable action plans. Here as elsewhere they have once again ignored the teachings of their religion and their Prophet (SAAS) and their ability to find a solution by *Ijtehad* to a problem whose solution is a must. They should recognise and believe that:

'THE MOSQUE ITSELF SHOULD BE THE BASE FOR THE GLOBAL ISLAMIC REVIVAL.'

This institution already exists and is constantly expanding. If the Muslims put further resources into it and a substantial portion of their effort then they can rapidly change the situation of the *Ummah* which will then become a formidable force to do good - *Maruf* and prevent evil - *Munkar*.

Ijtehad: Exertion. A logical deduction of a Muslim learned man of Islam. It is one of the major sources of Islamic jurisprudence.

Here is what needs to be done urgently:-

A. Structure of the Mosque.

A1. A mosque should be set up in every community of Muslims West or East (wherever there is a gap it should be filled up).

A2. Existing mosques should be expanded and newer ones should be built, where possible, allowing for the provision of spaces suitable for use as library, meeting hall, recreation hall, children's creche and women's hall. A room for interactive video machines and a computer with communication links, fax cards and printer must be made available. These would enable the mosque to teach the Qur'an, Arabic language, Muslim history, current affairs, and to provide tuition as well as maintain direct local and international communications. A small kitchen and refreshment area and adequate toilet facilities are essential. Some space should be allocated for local social/community work office. If the main mosque building cannot accommodate all this then suitable adjacent or nearby property/ies should be purchased/rented.

B. Organisation and daily operation of the Mosque.

B1. The *Imam* must be a well educated person, preferably locally educated. This means that the *Imam* in UK and America must be at least a graduate of secular education either in English or another subject; must know Arabic language and must have thorough grounding in Islam. Ideally he should have dual qualifications both in religious studies and secular subjects. He must be a good organiser, speaker and dedicated. The *Imam* should be paid well and provided with the necessary benefits of accommodation,

pension etc. In larger communities the *Imam* might require
one or two assistants either part or full time.

B2. The committee of the mosque should be constituted
from those members of the local community who are
respected for their piety and character and have some record
of achievement in business, education, profession or
community work.

B3. The first task of the mosque must be to prepare a
database, properly designed, of all the local Muslims and
their families who reside in their catchment area. This
should include local Muslim businesses and Muslims
working in the area but who do not live in the area. Local
mosques should co-ordinate to ensure that this data is not
duplicated.

B4. The various mini organisations or sub-committees
within the mosque for teaching, counselling, social work
should be organised under the leadership of the best and most
suitable persons from the local community.

B5. The mosque must carry out regular social welfare and
dawah work in the local community both Muslims and non-
Muslims. It is not only an Islamic duty but the only way to
practically demonstrate to non-Muslims that Islam teaches
care, concern and welfare of the neighbourhood specially the
elderly, disabled and disadvantaged. It is also a sound
training in character building for young Muslims who should
be actively involved in such work.

B6. Every Muslim family in the community must be made
to feel that they belong to the mosque and the mosque
belongs to them. The database of addresses will enable the
mosque committee to constantly monitor the welfare of the
neighbourhood. Women and children must be encouraged to

Dawah: Call, invitation. Duty of Muslims to invite others to the straight path of Islam.

use the mosque and must be taught to respect the sanctity of the mosque. Every effort should be made to ensure that the mosque becomes the focal point of the local Muslim community.

B7. Mosques in an area, region or country should unite in some form of organisation or federation to co-ordinate their activities and share knowledge and experiences of teaching, professional fund raising, community work etc. They should cut out local politics and reduce other political activities that are not of any direct benefit to Muslims. They should concentrate on religious, educational, social and community welfare work. Special attention must be paid to Muslim current affairs and all those issues that affect Muslims.

A well run, well-managed mosque will ensure good relations with the people of other faith and will give a sense of confidence to local Muslims and non-Muslims that in an emergency they can depend on the mosque for help and support.

The above if repeated in the local community of Muslims, throughout the West and the East will have in no time at all a global impact on Muslims at very little cost in terms of money and organisational effort since the foundation is already there. Muslims will also be able to communicate and co-ordinate, through their local mosque, *Imam* and committee on a global scale on issues that affect their religion and communities. A mosque is Allah's House and not the headquarters of a local party or organisation that Muslims will quibble, differ, or argue about the above aims. A mosque as Allah's House belongs to the community of Muslims. No person, not even one who has contributed all the money to build it can have a lien on a mosque.

It is noted that the above aims cannot at present be fully realised in some places of conflict such as Bosnia and Kashmir. In some other countries dictatorial regimes are locking up the mosques in between prayer times. They are doing so because they realise the power of the mosque and its ability to revive the faith of Muslims. In such exceptions as mentioned here a separate and different solution is needed. The Qur'an and *sunnah* do give guidance for solving such problems.

Other organisations and Mosques.

The comments made above about plethora of Muslim organisations do not apply to large well managed Muslim organisations. Many large well managed and well funded Muslim organisations are badly needed everywhere specially in Europe and America. They are our intellectual front line against attacks on Islam and Muslims. Some Muslim organisations in Europe and America provide the most resolute and powerful stand and are the only spokesmen against corrupt rulers and tyrant regimes. This is because of their rapidly growing strength in the intellectual, technical and organisational fields together with their commitment to Islam and their determination to lead a balanced social and moral life under difficult conditions. All such organisations whose activities are within the guidelines of the Qur'an and *sunnah* deserve every Muslim's whole-hearted support. They must be allowed to use the local institution of the mosque to get them rapidly known throughout the country in every Muslim home.

Muslims with intellect and energy should first consider assisting established organisations rather than setting up newer ones. This will have the effect of concentrating larger resources where maximum results can be achieved.

Differences in personality, approach and methodology should not be a cause of mutual conflict and confrontation between Muslim organisations and their leaders. After all the aim is one though the approach and route are diverse.

Halal and Haram

In Islam *halal* means lawful and permissible. *Haram* means unlawful and prohibited. In matters as to what was lawful and what was prohibited, people had gone astray before the advent of Islam. This happened partly because of ignorance but mostly by chopping and changing Allah's laws as revealed to previous peoples of the book. They permitted many impure and harmful things and prohibited many things that were pure and good. At the time when Islam came the error, confusion and deviation in respect of what was *halal* and what was *haram* was widespread. One of Islam's great accomplishments was not only to address this problem in depth but to redress it as well. Islam established, through Divine guidance and the Prophet's (SAAS) *sunnah*, legal principles and measures to clarify and rectify this matter. The basic principles of Qur'an and *sunnah* were then made the determining criteria or the core rules on which the question of what is *halal* and what is *haram* are based. And to this day, despite advances in man's knowledge, environment and abundance of variety the principle works.

The basic principle regarding *halal* is that every act or transaction is allowed unless it is prohibited. This principle emphasises growth and development and not restriction, narrowness and hardness.

With regard to *haram* everything that is destructive for a person as an individual, his society and his environment - destruction and harmful in the physical, mental and spiritual sense - is regarded as *haram* or forbidden.

It is important to reflect here that the *shari'ah*, in laying down the law of *halal* and *haram* conforms to human nature and is in tune with it. The laws of *halal* and *haram* and the sanctions are all meant to create the conditions under which man can preserve and safeguard all that is noble and just from all that is false, destructive and vicious. There are categories of *halal* divided into *fard* or compulsory, *mustahabb* or recommended, *mubaah* or tolerated, *makruh* or disliked. As far as *haram* is concerned there are basic principles governing various prohibitions.

Muslims must be aware that there are some areas where there are no precise pronouncements in the *shari'ah*. It is advisable to avoid the doubtful areas on the principle that when in doubt leave it out. Otherwise it may lead in the end to what is unlawful. A Muslim should not place oneself in situations of temptation or go near to what is clearly prohibited.

Now let us examine some Islamic principles and applications of *halal* and *haram*, same for the last 1400 years by comparing it to what the Western secular government or the Catholic Church has allowed or prohibited. Islam has prohibited adultery, fornication and homosexuality but has encouraged lawful marriage. Sex is a natural desire and marriage the most appropriate means to fulfil it. The Catholic Church prohibits marriage for its clergy. The secular society and other churches do not object to it. Some Western secular governments have made homosexuality and abortion lawful with proper legislation but the Catholic church is against it. President Clinton of of the United States is for abortion and homosexuality but Pope Paul of Rome is against it. What a mockery and mix-up of morals and law, right and wrong. We are now suffering, as a result of laxity of morals, on a world-wide basis, from the scourge of Aids. And so many American families have to live with the shame, guilt and suffering inflicted on them by the Catholic priests through widespread child abuse. This was exposed by the recent extensive media publicity although the problem was old but hidden for centuries.   All because of unnatural laws prohibited by one Christian leader and   promoted by another.   The Jews also have quite a clever law.   They can lend money to fellow Jews but only without interest.   But they can charge interest and indulge in usury for lending to all others.   This has now led to   world wide interest based systems thanks to the power and dominance of Jews in money matters.   The misery inflicted on small businessmen who had to borrow for legitimate business enterprises from banks but who could not, due to recession and   despite their best efforts   pay back the loans are there for all to see.   The adverse effects of interest based lending on South America and Africa are devastating.   Similarly the adverse effect on society of alcoholism, breakdown of home and family life, gambling and financial laxity are too numerous to mention.   There are no   serious prohibitions or accountability now - religious or secular on violating many basic moral values.   On the contrary we   are being vigorously encouraged   for ever greater indulgence.   In some countries society is now reaching breaking point and the time is not far for local time bombs to start exploding!

Islam forbids all interest based transactions.   Alcohol, gambling and sexual perversion are strictly forbidden in Islam and are considered *haram* acts.   It would be inconceivable in an Islamic society for the daughter-in-law of the Queen, wife of a Prince and mother of two children to have her toes sucked by her financial adviser in a state of nakedness.   To add insult to injury her photographs are then displayed for the morbid pleasure of the public in the name of freedom of press.   And then they are all making loud claims to be a Christian and civilised society.   Surely it is nothing less than perversion in the name of secular civilisation!

Men in Islam

Many articles, booklets and books have been written about 'Women in Islam' but we have seen none about 'Men in Islam.' We believe it is right that this imbalance is balanced. Islam enjoins some responsibilities on men, some on women and many joint responsibilities on both of them.

If Islam and Muslims are to succeed then Muslim men must examine their role and conduct in the light of Islamic teachings and the needs and requirements of the time. Let us examine Muslim men's role, duties and performance against a check list.

1.   Men as head of family.

1.1   Are they discharging their duty towards their family in accordance with the Commandments of Allah (SWT) and His Messenger (SAAS)?   Are they performing *salah* and adhering to the other basic duties of Islam and ensuring that their spouse and children do the same?

1.2   Are they by their conduct and their piety setting an example of proper Muslim conduct and Muslim manners at home?   Children learn by example.   If the father does not practice Islam he would not be in a position to ask his wife and children to do so.   If the children learn Islam elsewhere and have a non-practising father their close relationship with him is bound to suffer.

1.3   Are they ensuring as head of their family that their wives and daughters wear *hijab* and express through their dress and conduct Islamic values?   Our research indicates that in some Muslim households while mother, daughter and son want to be better and more practising Muslims, some men, as fathers and husbands are actually preventing or discouraging them to do so.

Hijab: Cover, wrap, Muslim woman's veil.

1.4   Are they ensuring both the religious and secular education of their children and are they making the necessary sacrifices for it? The greatest asset of the *Ummah* are its young. Only a well brought up and well educated or skill trained Muslim can hope to be an asset; others may well prove to be a liability.

1.5   Although giving advice is easy than implementing it we nevertheless feel that we must bring to the attention of our readers an important issue. This involves the problem faced by working Muslim mothers when their children are still young and are left with baby-sitters or in some form of care. It is very difficult to draw the line between right and wrong as each family's needs and financial circumstances will differ. But it can be safely said that if by lowering their material expectations and sticking to necessities rather than working for luxuries Muslim women can afford to stay at home and look after their children, then they must do so. The Qur'an and *sunnah* have both exalted the role of motherhood above all else and there is great deal of Divine wisdom in it. One can see the adverse effects on many children in the West where the mother is also a career woman. We deal with some alternatives available to working Muslim mothers in our essay on 'Women in Islam.'

2.   Men as members of community.

2.1   A Muslim's conduct in the local community, in the wider circle of friends and acquaintances, at educational establishments, work place and other gatherings is a reflection on Islam. A Muslim man has certain rules of behaviour with neighbours, at work place, in the conduct of business and in other group situations. Men as members of the Islamic community and as heads of their family should examine their conduct in the light of the Qur'anic injunction:

"Let there be a community (or Ummah) among you, advocating what is good, demanding what is right, and eradicating what is wrong. These are indeed the successful."
(Surah Al-i-Imran 3:104)

Individual conduct determines family and group conduct, local community conduct and global *Ummah* conduct. Successful *dawah* to non-Muslims cannot be accomplished in any community anywhere if the conduct of Muslims in that community is questionable.

2.2 It is incumbent on every Muslim man to devote a small portion of his time on local community, local charity and local *dawah* work. This may include assisting any active Muslim organisation or institution, helping at the local mosque or *madrasah*, local charity or *dars* group and involvement in local play or social group. This can be extended to providing free tuition to local Muslims by qualified and trained teachers or other educated Muslims. One should endeavour to do whatever is within one's capacity. This active and grassroots work is essential for the improvement of the Muslim community and to make them better and responsible members of society. Most of us are very busy in trying to make a living but where there is a will some spare time can be found.

Watching television and reading newspaper reports about Bosnia, Kashmir and Palestine is not enough. Some form of active involvement on a continuing basis by every Muslim is necessary, deeper involvement by more committed Muslims is a must.

The Qur'an and *hadith* enjoin on men responsibility towards family, friends and neighbours, the local community

---

Madrasah: A religious school associated with a mosque; the lower grades of a secondary school in Muslim countries.

and the *Ummah*. All men will have to answer before Allah (SWT) how they discharged this obligation on the day of judgement. This is an issue that affects the very health and survival of Muslims and cannot be avoided. The revival of their faith, the renewing of their resolve, the strengthening and improvement of their situation can never be achieved unless all Muslim men can honestly and truly answer most if not all of the questions posed above in an affirmative manner.

The establishment of Islamic states, the educational and technical advancement of Muslims, the general improvement in their situation can only be achieved if Muslim men develop and improve themselves as individuals, families, communities until they become a model *Ummah*. It will then be possible to change everything and influence anyone. This is a difficult task but there are no soft options available.

The following is the prayer for righteous men from the Qur'an:

"...Our Lord! Grant unto us wives and offspring who will be the joy and the comfort of our eyes, and guide us to be models of righteousness."
(Surah Furqan 25:74)

Women in Islam

A great deal of published material is now available on this subject. We do not wish to repeat more of the same. We think that the debate on Women's place in Islam is now over. The time has come to examine, in a practical manner, how can the Muslimahs contribute for the betterment of the *Ummah* as mother, wife, daughter and as an active member of the Muslim community. The question is not what is her role, the urgent issue is how best she can discharge that role.

1. General.

There is now some consensus among Muslims that the role of our women is both important and wide ranging in the modern world. There is also growing consensus and confidence that it is now possible for Muslim women to remain good Muslimahs and be able to discharge most of the duties and cope with most of the demands made on them by the present day society. At no time in Muslim history except during the time of the Prophet (SAAS) the role of Muslim women has been of greater importance than it is today. On a local level this role has been greater in some Muslim countries at different times in history but never a greater global demand was made on the Muslimahs. This applies to the ordinary Muslim women, the professional and educated Muslim women, the rich Muslim women including princesses and sheikhas and the influential Muslim women in politics, teaching, business or as wives of influential Muslims. Let us examine some situations and make some recommendations and action plans. There is no single panacea for the many problems facing Muslims but that should not deter us from looking for solutions and for relying on Allah's (SWT) help.

2. Muslim Women's identity.

Religious and cultural identity distinguishes one people from another. One of the great strengths of Western culture is that it gives in Western dress some distinct identity to Western woman whether she is in bikini, skirt, trouser or dress. Muslim women vary in their style of dress depending on the part of the world they live, but there is still two Islamic rules that promote and sustain their common identity. It is the *hijab* and the modesty of their dress as prescribed by their religion that achieves this. *Hijab* can truly be said to be the identifying symbol of the world wide Muslimahs. It is sad and very degrading to see so many educated Muslim women not wearing *hijab* and adopting the vulgar Western dress. *Hijab* is the pre-requisite to fulfil the requirements of modesty of dress required by Allah (SWT) from all Muslimahs.

Hijab and a modest style of Islamic dress represents female modesty and respectability and asserts Muslim women's dignity and self-esteem in a public manner. Western dress often symbolises a permissible lifestyle and an invitation to sexual and other harassment. Therefore every Muslim woman must feel proud in wearing *hijab* and must pay special attention to modesty of dress and ornament in public.

Muslim women were given an exalted status and many rights by Islam fourteen hundred years ago. Some of these rights have been granted to Western women after a great deal of struggle only recently. The question now arises as to what the modern Muslimah is doing to express her gratitude to Allah (SWT) for His favours to her. A question can be posed to every Muslim woman **'don't ask what Islam can do for you; ask what you can do for Islam?'** In dressing

---

Hijab: Cover, wrap, Muslim woman's veil.

themselves in an Islamic manner a Muslim woman is not only following Allah's (SWT) Commandments but is also expressing gratitude to her Creator. Therefore she must feel pride and pleasure in dressing strictly according to the Islamic code. Some Muslim women think that Western dress and haircut makes them advanced and progressive. In fact this is untrue. Muslim women who adopt this Western dress code and show-off hair look totally out of place. Contrary to popular belief majority of people in the West don't think much of these women.

3. Education and training of Muslim women.

Every Muslimah should aim to obtain the highest possible education including advanced education and training in the professions commensurate with her abilities. This is over and above her thorough education and study of Qur'an, *hadith*, Muslim literature, culture, history and on-going involvement with Muslim current affairs. Every type of education and training is permissible for the Muslimah unless it is manifestly *haram* or may expose her to undignified and unlawful situations. However, certain professions are more suitable and desirable for women. These are teaching, law, accountancy, journalism, information technology, medical science specialising in women and children, research based careers such as scientists, consultants. Those who cannot pursue higher education for any reason must undergo some vocational or skill training. These can include typing, word-processing, nursing, tailoring and hundreds of other *halal* occupations and hobbies for which suitable skill training is available. Education is no longer the privilege of the few. Those Muslim elders or leaders who still propagate that women do not need education are wrong and backward.

4. Muslim women's role as wife and mother.

The Muslim woman's role and duties as wife and mother has not changed at all in the last fourteen hundred years. Both Qur'an and *hadith* are very clear about the sanctity of this role. Islam attaches greater importance to the role of a Muslim woman as wife and particularly as mother compared to all her other roles. Indeed her role as a career woman even when she is well educated and qualified cannot take priority over her role as mother while her children are young. A great deal of careful planning, understanding and compromise is essential as there may arise situations where important decisions and choices must be made when children and careers clash. The golden rule for the Muslimah here is to follow Islam in the bringing up of her children rather than continue with her career. In many cases it may be possible for some women to combine part time work or to work from home. For accountants, lawyers, writers, journalists, computer specialists, home workers and members of some other professions it may be possible to work from home. It is not an ideal solution but a preferable course for those women who must keep intellectually busy or need to earn some extra money when their children are young. It should be noted that the duty of imparting early religious education to her children and instilling in them Islamic values and pride in being Muslims rests to a large extent on Muslim mothers.

Once children are grown the Muslimah can go back to her job or career after a refresher course or re-training.

5. Muslim women Vs local community/dars and social activities.

Muslims are now fortunate to have mosques and institutions for the teaching of Qur'an and Islam everywhere in the West. Plenty of books, teaching aids are also available. There are also *dars* and other group activities going on all the time. It is important for Muslim women of all ages to actively involve themselves in these activities and to play a role suitable to their education and availability. Educated Muslim women should help their less educated sisters. Those who have more time should profitably employ it on local social work, teaching, lecturing, counselling, fund raising. All this makes for a vibrant and well adjusted community.

6. Muslim women's role outside home.

A Muslim woman's conduct outside her home is a reflection on her faith and virtue, her family and on Islam. It cannot be overemphasised that once outside home she is the very embodiment of 'living Islam'. She must distinguish between *halal* and *haram*, right and wrong, proper and improper in accordance with the teachings of Islam and not the dictates of custom or fashion. The Muslimah as sister, daughter, wife and mother closely holds her family together and instils in them high standards of character and behaviour by her own example.

7. A practical way for enhancing local Muslim unity and social contact.

We would like to mention here one of the ways of enhancing local unity, social contact and sharing of ideas and problems that has been successfully working with excellent results in a part of England. The idea originated from two local women that between ten to twenty Muslim families should get together regularly once every month. They got together twelve families who gathered, for the first few months, taking turns in each other's houses. Each family cooked some food and brought it to the designated house. All members of the family got together. The gathering was on the last Saturday of each month between 7 to 10 pm. Food was shared. The separate male and female groups discussed current problems, education and community matters, bringing up of children. Children made friends and shared their school and sports news and experiences. They also discussed religion and other subjects. Brief talks were given on important issues by different persons and followed by discussions. Such was the initial success of this activity that this group have now obtained, through the generosity of a local charity, the regular use of a public hall once a month. This hall has space for lectures, games and some sports facilities. The cost of the hall is negligible. We believe Muslims everywhere should organise such a get-together. There could be many groups in the same locality. The social, cultural and other benefits are enormous compared to the time and effort expended. Ideally the groups should be minimum ten and maximum twenty. Once the group is formed and started someone on its behalf can contact the local council for the use of a hall, a youth or recreation centre. Local charitable organisations may also help. We think it is a wonderful idea for gaining educational, social and religious benefits on a regular basis.

8. Conclusion.

Our emphasis on education and training of Muslimahs is not a licence to ignore her *tarbiyah* in family management and acquisition of skills for running her home. It must remain the first priority in all homes. Education and training should enhance a Muslimah's ability to manage her home, children and extended family much better than an uneducated person. Education up to O level/Matriculation with an extended syllabus of religious education must be made compulsory for all young men and women in all Muslim countries. It has been estimated by some researchers that the literacy level of the Jews is ninety-six per cent while that of the *Ummah* is no more than twenty-five percent. This gap is alarming!

Hijab

Hijab for the purposes of our article means head cover and wrapping worn by Muslim women. The broader meaning of *hijab* is cover, wrap, drape, woman's veil, partition, barrier. The subject of *hijab* for Muslim women in itself is not a matter of controversy whether the country is Saudi Arabia, Malaysia or America, whether the women cover head and face or head only. We are concerned here with the minimum head cover. The current revival of Islam, particularly among young people has led to certain problems in the wearing of *hijab* in the West and in some secular Muslim countries. The following scenarios can be observed:

In the West.
There is some controversy at educational institutions, work places, offices and factories on the wearing of *hijab* by Muslim women - refer to the case of the French school where Muslim girls were prevented from wearing *hijab*. There is also tension in some Muslim homes in Europe and America on the issue of *hijab*. The grown up daughters, consistent with current Islamic revival, have started wearing *hijab* against the wishes of their parents. In some cases mummy does not wear *hijab* but the daughter does!

In Muslim Countries.
The revival of Islam has led many women particularly younger and educated women in countries such as Egypt, Algeria and Morocco into wearing *hijab*. Some countries are discouraging this trend through secular media, others have gone as far as to ban it by the force of law - at least from government offices and public areas.

The media in the West has turned its propaganda

machine to label this revival to wear *hijab* as 'Islamic fundamentalism'.

Nowhere Islam has described the wearing *hijab* as an act of fundamentalism. Islam has no concept of fundamentalism as propagated by the West and *hijab* is not a part of it. *Hijab* is part of an obligatory requirement made on Muslim women by an overall Divine Commandment towards guarding their modesty and chastity. One interpretation of what constitutes modesty of dress is long skirt, loose coat and head scarf. This is minimum requirement. The other is full covering including the face. Modesty in dress in public has profound social, cultural and spiritual significance. It is one of the basic injunctions of Islam on the principle that prevention is better than cure, specially in areas of moral decay of society. Many Qur'anic injunctions are on this basis and with this objective in mind. They have been further supplemented by the Prophet's *sunnah.* It is also one of the reasons among others for the Muslim's claim that if Islamic principles are applied many evils of modern societies such as Aids, alcoholism, ruin through gambling, mental disease and discontent, breakdown of family life and sexual perversion can be substantially reduced and in some cases eliminated.

Why has Islam made wearing of *hijab* by Muslim women compulsory while the present day Christian society accepts women's nakedness as a matter of routine? Is the God of Muslims backward? Such questions do perplex many minds particularly young Muslim minds. What follows is an attempt to provide some answers.

● Many societies in the past have observed standards of decent conduct in segregating women. They took steps to protect the virtue and honour of their women folk through proper clothing. They also prevented irregular meeting and mixing of sexes.

● Most Christian women of the past wore some form of *hijab*. Religious and other paintings of the past show women including the virgin Mary wearing some form of head cover. Women can still be seen wearing head cover in the rural areas of Eastern Europe.

● Over the centuries the Catholics and other churches have been dispensing new rules, chopping and changing others to suit the vagaries of taste, time and fashion. The church is man - controlled with ever changing man - made rules. With the separation of church from government and rapid decline in morality these rules became more and more lax to deal with moral and social problems of Christians in particular and mankind in general. There is nothing old fashioned about basic morality and decency. Such values are everlasting.

● Islamic rules on all basic issues, particularly social and moral issues, are Divine rules. Unlike human wisdom, Divine wisdom does not change from time to time, place to place by its very definition. The basic laws, Commandments and rules given to Muhammad (SAAS) fourteen hundred years ago were applicable then, are applicable now and will remain applicable till the end of the world.

The wearing of *hijab* by Muslim women is one of these basic laws confirmed by a broad Divine Commandment requiring modesty of dress, ornament and proper behaviour from them to protect their chastity and dignity.
The original Command is as follows:

> *"O Prophet! Tell your wives and daughters, and the*
> *believing women, that they cast their outer garments over*
> *their persons (when outside their homes): that is most*
> *convenient, that they should be known (as such) and not*
> *molested. And Allah is indeed most Forgiving, Most*
> *Merciful."*
> (Surah Ahzab 33:59)

A further and general Commandment giving Divine guidance on the subject of modesty in dress and required behaviour is given in the Qur'an in the following verse:

> *"Say to the believing women that they should lower their*
> *gaze and guard their modesty; that they should not display*
> *their beauty and ornaments except that which is displayed*
> *of itself, and to draw their veils over their bosoms and not*
> *to display their beauty (and ornaments) except to their*
> *husbands, their fathers, their husband's fathers, their sons,*
> *their sister's sons, or their women or their slaves whom*
> *their right hands possess, or male servants free of physical*
> *needs, or small children who have not attained knowledge*
> *of sex matters; and that they should not strike their feet on*
> *the ground in order to draw attention to their hidden*
> *ornaments. And O you Believers! Turn you all together*
> *towards Allah that you may attain true success."*
> (Surah Nur 24:31)

It is clear from the above verses that the wearing of *hijab* is essential if Muslim women are to comply with the requirements of the above verses. Only then can a Muslim woman reflect the modesty of her dress. It is a preventive measure to check the moral decay of society, to prevent adultery, and other social ills of the society. *Hijab* also gives inner and outer dignity to women. Even non-Muslims in the

West respect a woman with *hijab*. Such a woman in *hijab* can carry out all her duties and responsibilities as a student, as an office or manual worker or as a professional with dignity and authority whether she is in East or West. It also provides a special and distinctive cultural identity to Muslim women of which they should be proud.

In Saudi Arabia and some other Arab countries women cover both their face and hand. But it is perfectly proper and within Islamic rules not to cover face and hands. Islam is not a religion of hardship or rigidity since the purpose of *hijab* is to protect modesty and chastity not to make it difficult for Muslim women to follow their professions or vocations. Islam attaches a great deal of importance to marriage, children, motherhood and family life. It nevertheless gives complete freedom to women to get higher education, and acquire professional qualifications and training. The only rules to follow here are those laid down by Islam which set standards and boundaries of decency, morality and duty. *Hijab* is one such boundary.

There is no shame in Muslim women wearing *hijab* in any country, in any place, at any time. The true shame is on Muslim women who do not wear *hijab*. Muslim women who ignore the religious, cultural and modesty rules of their religion and adopt the fashionable and immodest ways of the West are neither accepted by the West nor respected by Muslims or non-Muslims.

Islamic System of Morality

Morality has been defined in the dictionary as principles of good behaviour conforming to moral principles, goodness and rightness. This definition is not comprehensive enough for Muslims. Good behaviour without faith in the Unity of Allah (SWT) and without good intention -*niya*- is of little merit. The gist of Islamic morality is summed up in the following Qur'anic verse:

"...Enjoin what is Just, and forbid what is wrong..."
(Surah Luqman 31:17)

General.
Islam is a natural, proper and balanced way of life. It follows the middle path. It neither allows nor recommends any extremes. The religion of Islam has not been made unbearable for its followers. It does not have strict rules and rituals but at the same time it does not adopt laxity and compromise by ignoring what is palatable and not forbidding what is manifestly wrong and harmful.

To lead a natural, honest, proper and balanced life, one needs laws, rules, instructions and guidance in a comprehensive form. Islam provides these laws, rules, instructions and guidance covering all aspects of life.

Islamic rules of morality are based on the following principles:

⊓ **Faith** in Allah (SWT). The Creator is deemed to be the source of all virtue, goodness, truth and guidance.

⊓ **Man** as Allah's vicegerent. Man by nature is deemed to be good although some among men (men/man refer to both male and female) are bound to err and commit sins.

This is because man has not been created perfect like angels who are not capable of committing sins.

□ **Rules** laid down by Allah (SWT). They are essential to distinguish right and wrong and at the same time are neither unbearable nor so lax as to make everything enjoyable and easy without any accountability.

□ **Balance** (neither one extreme or the other), moderation and practicality which encourage higher standards of conduct and morality.

□ **The process** of natural selection means that all things are permissible unless strictly forbidden by Allah (SWT) and a man of faith will not question His wisdom in forbidding it.

□ **The ultimate responsibility** of man is to Allah (SWT) in following His moral Commandments.

Having accepted the basic principles the next aspect of morality in Islam is its practical application to man's daily life.

It is a fundamental doctrine in Islam that a Muslim cannot be expected to behave morally and properly who does not follow the practices of the basic pillars of Islam. This is because virtuous conduct and moral behaviour flow from it. The pillars of Islam are:

1. To bear witness to Allah's Oneness and to be constantly aware of Him; to believe in Muhammad (SAAS) as his last Messenger, *shahadah.*
2. To observe daily prayers, *salah.*
3. To pay, where applicable, the *zakah* (religious tax).

4. To keep the fast of *Ramadan*.
5. To perform *hajj,* (pilgrimage to Makkah) if he can afford it, at least once in his lifetime.

After these basic requirements a Muslim's behaviour and conduct with parents, children, relatives, friends   and neighbours must be in accordance with the Commandments of Allah (SWT). A Muslim's conduct in business, in the affairs of his family, his conduct in the wider community with both Muslims and non-Muslims must be in conformity with the Islamic principles. Islamic rules are universal. They do not have exceptions and exemptions based on location, status, class, colour or origin.

A Muslim must know how to distinguish between *halal* and *haram,* right and wrong in order to implement in practice the Qur'anic injunction: 'Enjoin what is just and forbid what is wrong.' Forbidding evil as mentioned here has broad meaning since one is under obligation to forbid evil by word of mouth, by the written word and by physical action. Similarly enjoining what is just means in a broad sense doing *dawah* work and spreading the word of Allah (SWT), the virtue and beauty of Islam to a wider community. The Qur'an has summed up the grounds, the philosophy and the basis of morality in one of the most moving and profound messages as follows. It is just one of the many passages from the Qur'an.

"O Children of Adam! Wear your beautiful apparel at
every time and place of prayer; eat and drink, but waste not
by excess, for Allah loves not the wasters. Say: 'Who has
forbidden the beautiful gifts of Allah, which he has
produced for His servants and the things clean and pure
(which He has provided) for sustenance?' Say: 'They are,
in the life of this world, for those who believe, (and) purely

for them on the Day of Judgement.' Thus do we explain the signs in detail for those who understand. Say: 'The things that my Lord indeed forbidden are: shameful deeds, whether open or secret, sins and trespasses against truth or reason; assigning of partners to Allah for which He has given no authority and saying things about Allah of which you have no knowledge."
(Surah Araaf 7:31-33)

Morality must be expressed in daily conduct such as making of promises and returning trusts, and in business dealings. The following verse of the Qur'an refers to this;

"Give full measure and be not of those who cause others to lose. And weigh with an equal balance. And defraud not people of their things, and commit no corruption in the land."
(Surah Shuaraa 26:181-183)

The neglect of morality has turned a great country like the United States of America into the sink hole of violence and sexual abandon. They may be fit to be sheriffs of Dodge city but not quite the New World Order. The United States needs an urgent re-think and a social Marshall Plan for improvement in its society and government both on a national as well as international scale in areas covering morality, violence, justice and equality.

Islamic Manners toward Parents and Relatives

The basic unit of the society is family and family consists of parents, children, relatives. Western civilisation and its moral and cultural values have helped to damage the family base structure. The family life in the West is ruined. The sanctity of relations, care and concern by the young for their older parents is fast disappearing. High percentage of divorce, the large number of unmarried mothers, the ambitions of women to follow careers rather than motherhood, the material greed to keep up with the Jones's has all contributed to the destruction of the family unit in the West.

The first step in saving any society is to establish the family on the right footing. Islam has provided an elaborate set of instructions and guidance for establishing and preserving a sound family life.

In Islam the highest right over mankind is that of Allah (SWT). Following this is the domestic and family life in which parents are entitled to the highest place and foremost rights. Behaviour with and treatment of parents encompasses obedience, gratitude, tolerance and service to them. This is required both in their life time, specially in their old age and also after their death. After parents are the rights of other relatives both on the paternal as well as the maternal side. Other distant relatives, though on a lesser degree compared to one's parents, also have rights.

Kindness and obedience to parents.

The following verse of the Qur'an illustrates its importance.

"Thy Lord hath decreed that ye worship none but Him,
And that ye be kind To parents. Whether one or both of
them attain old age in thy life, say not to them a word of
contempt, nor repel them, but address them in terms of
honour. "
(Surah Al-Isra 17:23)

Kindness in old age is strongly recommended. It is at this time that one can be tempted to snigger at parents. Both patience and wisdom are needed to handle a difficult situation caused by the old age and frailty of parents.

Gratitude towards parents.

Be grateful to your parents. It is the first principle of good manners and acknowledgement of the debt for all the acts of kindness that one has received from parents. This debt of parents must be repaid in greater measure in kindness, concern for their welfare and by active involvement in looking after them.

"And We have enjoined on man goodness towards his
parents. His mother bore him by bearing strain upon
strain, and his utter dependence on her lasted two years.
Hence, O Man, be grateful to Me and to your Parents (and
remember that) with Me is all journey's end. "
(Surah Luqman 31:14)

Tolerance towards parents.

It is the duty of all Muslims to please their parents and not to do anything to hurt their feelings, particularly when they get old and are easily angered or irritated.

"And, out of kindness, lower to them the wing of humility, and say: "My Lord! Bestow on them Thy Mercy even as they cherished me in childhood."
(Surah Al-Isra 17:24)

Even if parents or one them are non-Muslims they are to be treated well and all courtesy shown to them. Only obedience in matters of religion is to be refused and they are not to be followed if they ask their children to associate anyone with Allah (SWT) or to commit an act of sin.

"We have enjoined on man kindness to parents: but if they (either of them) strive (to force) thee to join with Me (in worship) anything of which thou hast no knowledge, obey them not..."
(Surah Ankabuut 29:8)

Both the Qur'an and *hadith* have placed mothers in a very exalted position - much more deserving of kindness and service, than even one's father. The story of Al-Qaamah is an example and reminder to Muslims of the gravity of the sin of making a mother angry and the rewards of keeping her satisfaction and pleasure.

Duties to relations.

As mentioned before the Muslim family does not consist just of husband, wife and children but is extended to include relatives as well.

All Muslims are required to maintain a close and caring relationship with relatives. According to a saying of the Prophet, Muslims are required to visit relatives, enquire about their circumstance, spend on them and give them *sadaqah* if they are poor or in financial difficulties.

Sadaqah: Anything given in charity, almsgiving, freewill offering.

From the above we can see that the institution of the family consisting of parents, near and distant relatives is maintained by feelings of love, tenderness, by the Islamic laws of morality and decency and by practical measures of mutual assistance and support.

Strong, stable and healthy family units provide the foundation for strong stable and healthy communities and societies.

The absence of any such unified code and values as given in the Qur'an and *sunnah*, in the Western civilisation is the prime cause for the decay and decadence of their society which is now causing concern.

It is terribly sad to see so many children in the West whose parents are either divorced or the mother was never married in the first instance. Sometimes the children do not even know who their father is. They are deprived of parental love, affection and are often neglected by a harassed and overworked mother trying to juggle between money, time and her own social priorities.

A depressing trend where older people - grand fathers and grandmothers are being dumped into old people's homes or abandoned to live alone on their own can be observed.

This is an unlikely scenario in a Muslim family unless they have become totally Westernised and secularised and have adopted Western values or are facing abject poverty in a non-Islamic society.

Islamic Behaviour with Neighbours, Friends and Guests

Neighbours.

Islam lays down detailed rules and clear guidance for the 'code of conduct' one should apply in dealing with neighbours, guests and friends. In answer to the question as to 'what the rights of neighbours are?' - the Prophet (SAAS) replied as follows:

'Help him if he asks your help.
Give him relief if he seeks your relief.
Lend him if he needs a loan.
Show him concern if he is distressed.
Nurse him when he is ill.
Attend his funeral if he dies.
Congratulate him on his good news.
Sympathise with him if any calamity befall him.
Do not block his air by raising your building high without his permission.
Do not harass him.
Give him a share when you buy fruits, and if you do not give him, bring what you buy quietly and let not your children take them out to excite the jealousy of his children.'

This advice given fourteen hundred years ago can hardly be improved and is more relevant today than ever before. In many neighbourhoods, neighbours are now divided in rich and poor neighbours, which school their children go to, how many toys they have, which fashion designer clothes they wear and what exotic places they have visited on holiday. All this causes jealousy, tension and envy among neighbours.

The pressure of keeping up appearances is taking its toll. This makes in many cases, for very unpleasant co-existence and in some cases it is leading to a tiring and harassed existence. It is no wonder that one often hears about people in secure jobs and careers opting out of the system altogether in search of peace, quiet and simple living. This is now a social phenomena in Europe and America.

In big cities people live in blocks on the same street and in the same block of flats but many do not know one another. At least in Muslim neighbourhoods this should not be so. While Islam strongly recommends that a Muslim should respect the privacy of his neighbour it also requires him to be concerned in his welfare. A neighbour is not just the person who lives next door to you or in your own neighbourhood but also a fellow student, a fellow worker in office or factory or even a fellow-traveller on a journey.

'There is no distinction between a Muslim and a non-Muslim so far as human needs and rights of neighbourhood are concerned.'

The above advice of the Prophet (SAAS) applies to all neighbours.

Friends.
Regarding friendship the Qur'an says:

"The Believers men and women, are protectors one of another; they enjoin what is just, and forbid what is evil: they observe regular prayers, practice regular charity, and obey Allah and His Apostle..."
(Surah Tauba 9:71)

'A Muslim personifies love and affection. A Muslim who neither loves nor is loved in return by others, has no good in him.' (Mishkat)

The Prophet (SAAS) used to love his companions very much. Each one of his companions considered that he was the most beloved companion of the Prophet (SAAS). This is a very high standard of conduct on the part of the Prophet (SAAS).

There is well known saying that a person is known by the company he keeps. There is a further saying that to like and dislike the same things, that is indeed true friendship. Therefore a Muslim should consider as to what type of man is the person with whom his is going to forge close friendship. This means that when somebody would associate with a person, he is bound to be influenced by the sentiments and ideas of that person and he will have the same standard of likes and dislikes. If young or even older Muslims develop close friendship with wine drinking, disco dancing persons who associate Allah (SWT) with a son and holy ghost they are bound to be influenced by them. It is worse to make friends with people who engage in usury, gambling and prostitution. In such company a Muslim, particularly a young Muslim is unlikely to maintain his faith let alone enrich it. It is for this reason that the Prophet (SAAS) have advised Muslims to move in the company of virtuous persons only.

Muslims therefore should cultivate close friendships for the sake of Allah (SWT) alone. Allah's chosen servants are only those who unite with each other on the basis of their faith, and strive shoulder to shoulder with unity of heart and soul for the establishment and protection of Allah's religion , the religion of Islam. Friendship in Islam means friendship with virtuous people because friendship is for the sake of Allah (SWT). The best act of practical sincerity towards a friend that one can do is to try and improve his morals and better his prospects in the Hereafter even more than in this world.

Guests.

The *sunnah* of the Prophet (SAAS) tells us that the Prophet (SAAS) himself used to entertain his guests and he has said:

'Those who believe in Allah (SWT) and the Hereafter should be hospitable to their guests.' (Bukhari and Muslim)

Hospitality includes showing respect and cordiality, and arranging for the comfort and convenience of guests. The host should cheer his guest by pleasant conversation, introduce him to his intimate friends and serve him personally.

Islam stresses hospitality for guests and it is Muslim tradition not to get upset on the arrival of or any inconvenience caused by guests. Most Muslims entertain their guests with all the comfort, convenience and hospitality to the best of their means. Muslim hospitality of Arab and Central and South East Asian peoples have always been acknowledged.

Islamic Months

The Muslim calendar or Era is computed from the starting point of the year of the Prophet Muhammad's (SAAS) emigration *hijra* from Makkah to Madinah. It began on the 1st of Muharram of the first year of *hijra* IH or 15th July, 622 AD or CE.

The abbreviations:
H stands for *Hijra*,
AH stands for 'After *Hijra*.'
AD stands for 'Anno Domini' a Latin word meaning - 'In the year of our Lord.'
CE stands for 'Christian Era' or 'Common Era.'

Both AD and CE refer to what is known as Christian or Western calendar.

Muslim calendar or months are based on the Lunar System (dependent on the sighting of moon) and consists of twelve lunar months alternately of 30 and 29 days long beginning with the New Moon as shown below.

Muslim Months and Days:

months	days	months	days
Muharram	30	Rajab	30
Safar	29	Shaban	29
Rabi Al-Awwal	30	Ramadan	30
Rabi Al-Thani	29	Shawwal	29
Jumada Al-Ula	30	Dhu Al-Qaadah	30
Jumada Al-Thani	29	Dhu Al-Hijjah	29

The year has 354 days but the last month (Dhu Al-Hijjah) sometimes has an intercalated day bringing it to 30 days and making a total of 355 days for that year. Because of lunar calendar Muslim month of fasting, Eid and Hajj come every year at slightly different times. If Eid-ul-Adha was on 30th May 1993 (10th Dhu Al-Hijjah 1413 AH) this year then the next Eid-ul-Adha at the end of May/beginning of June will be in the year 2025 AD (1446 AH).

The Islamic months regress through all the seasons every thirty-two and a half years. It should be noted that it is not the month (Dhu Al-Hijjah for Eid-ul-Adha) but the season that changes. Eid-ul-Adha will always be on 10th Dhu Al-Hijjah and fasting will always be in the month of Ramadan but the season and weather will slightly change every year.

The Common Era or Christian Era calendar is based on the solar system. The formulas below can be used to convert Muslim *hijra* year to AD or CE year and vice-versa.

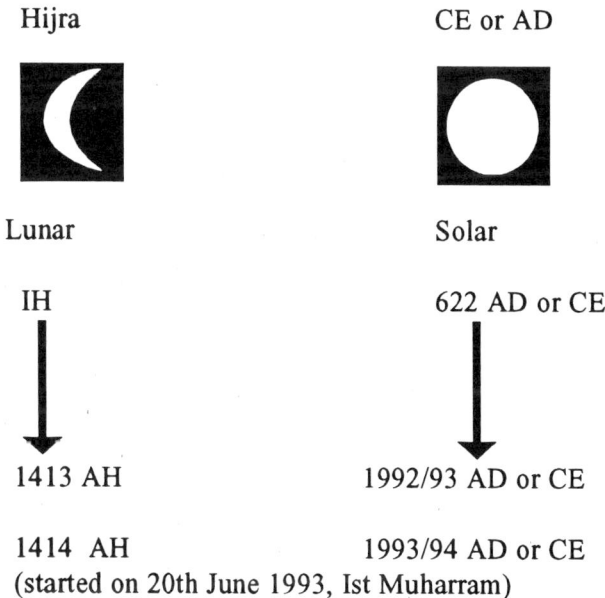

Hijra   CE or AD

Lunar   Solar

IH   622 AD or CE

1413 AH   1992/93 AD or CE

1414 AH   1993/94 AD or CE
(started on 20th June 1993, Ist Muharram)

To convert AD/CE 1150 to AH

$$AH = \frac{33}{32} (AD/CE -622)$$

$$1150\ AD = \frac{33}{32} (1150-622) = 544\ AH\ approx.$$

To convert AH 544 to AD or CE

$$AD = \frac{32}{33} (AH) + 622$$

Example 544 AH = $\frac{32}{33}$ x 544 + 622 = 1150 AD or CE approx.

Important milestones and festivals are associated with various Muslim months. Some are given below:

1st Muharram	Start of Muslim New Year
Miraj-un-Nabi	27th Rajab
1st Revelation of Qur'an	17th Ramadan
Eid-ul-Fitr	1st Shawwal
Fast of Arafat	9th Dhu Al-Hijjah
Prophet Muhammad's (SAAS) birthday	12th Rabi Al-Awwal
Ashura	10th Muharram
Change of Qibla	15th Shaban
Battle of Badr	17th Ramadan
Lailatul Qadr	21st to 28th night (odd nights of Ramadan)

Although the Islamic calendar dates from the first *hijra* year corresponding to about 622 AD, it is not possible to synchronise the dates of this calendar exactly with the

Christian calendar prior to 10 AH - 632 AD. This is because the pre-Islamic Pagan calendar was roughly luni-solar. The holy Prophet (SAAS) adopted the purely lunar calendar after the farewell pilgrimage in 10 AH Every date after 10 AH is exactly convertible into a corresponding date in any other standard calendar. The date of the actual *hijra* is now accepted as 22nd September 622 AD. But as the first month of the Arab year was and is Muharram the *hijra* year 1 is counted as beginning on 15th/16th July 622 AD (= 1 Muharram AH 1). It was during the Caliphate of Umar-ibn al-Khattab that the *hijri* era was started to be adopted in official documents, around 17/18 AH.

It must be noted that all Islamic dates and festivals are subject to sighting of the moon. The crescent is considered one of the Islamic symbols because Muslim year is measured by the lunar cycle.

For the benefit of the scientifically minded who may want to know what is meant by a lunar month we give some explanation. A lunar month is the time taken by the Moon to complete its journey round the Earth. The Moon is a satellite of the Earth; the Earth is a planet of the solar system. The Earth is twenty-five times as large as the Moon. The Moon takes 27 days, 7 hours and 3 minutes to travel round the Earth at a speed of 1km per second.

The First Four Caliphs

After the Prophet (SAAS), the first four caliphs of Islam - also known as the rightly guided caliphs - are held in high esteem by Muslims. The caliphate established after the Prophet's (SAAS) death lasted from 632 AD to 1258 AD. The period covered by the first four caliphs lasted from 632 AD to 661 AD, the Umayyad rule from 661 AD to 750 AD and the Abbasid rule from 750 AD to 1258 AD.

Details of their rule and the biography of the first four caliphs are available in many Islamic text books. Our purpose in writing about the first four caliphs here is to draw important lessons and inspirations and to see if they are relevant to current Muslim problems and aspirations. Muslims look back to this period with nostalgia particularly when they are writing or talking about Islamic government, justice, humility and quality of Islamic leadership. The greater part of this thirty year period provides an ideal of governance which is worth emulating. They may need some updating to suit modern times. But this updating is not of substance only of detail. The Prophet (SAAS) throughout his twenty-three years of Prophet-hood taught by example. These have become **model** examples for Muslims to follow. The four guided caliphs have also left a reservoir of wisdom and practical example for Muslims to emulate. We shall examine some salient features of this period and deduce any corresponding lessons.

1. The appointment of a Muslim ruler.
The first caliph Abu-Bakr (RA) was chosen by public consensus. Although the Prophet (SAAS) may have given

---

Caliph: Also referred as *Khalifah*. Successor, Vicegerent, Head of Muslim State. Man has been referred in the Qur'an as the caliph/*khalifah,* vicegerent of Allah (SWT).

some indirect sign of his preference for Abu-Bakr (RA) he never actually designated him as his successor. Two very important principles emerge from this. Firstly that the Prophet (SAAS) gave no preference to his closest relation Ali (RA). And secondly that he wanted the people to choose their own leader. This is an outstanding demonstration of Muhammad's (SAAS) guidance for future Muslims, rulers and ruled.

The second caliph Umar (RA) was appointed by Abu-Bakr (RA) after consultation with other senior and respected companions. This clearly shows a second method of appointing a Muslim ruler by due consultation with leading and respectable members of the *Ummah*. We know enough about the character and piety of Abu-Bakr (RA) to believe that he must have carried out proper and thorough consultations before appointing Umar (RA). In any case he could not have made a better choice.

The third caliph Uthman (RA) was appointed by yet another method. Before he died Umar (RA) prepared a short list of six names of the best and most pious companions, all fit to be his successor, and directed them to choose one from the list. This is a remarkably fair and proper way of selecting a successor, since at least four people must have consensus to choose someone from among them, or three if the chosen person abstains.

The last rightly guided caliph Ali (RA) was elected by the majority of the people of Madinah without any prior prompting by the previous caliph or the intervention of a selected group of pious companions.

We learn, from this brief example, four methods of selecting a Muslim ruler. The present day advance in science and technology, size and complexity of modern government do not alter a thing. By analogy and logical deduction it should be quite easy to transfer this selection process to any established or new Islamic state. We also have some guidance available from the Qur'an on this subject.

2. Upholding Allah's laws and Prophet's traditions.

2.1 Abu-Bakr's (RA) declaration of war against those who refused to pay *zakah* in the newly created Islamic state is a classic example of this. When Abu-Bakr (RA) came to power the Islamic state was in its infancy and the temptation to compromise might have been overwhelming. There were many problems to resolve in the new state. This courageous and righteous stand, against great odds, confirms the point that in matters where the very basic pillars of faith are at stake, there is no question of any compromise, since it would be in direct contravention of Allah's laws. Diplomacy, compromise and negotiations are understandable and within reason may be acceptable in matters of detail, at the lower levels, but never on basic beliefs and pillars of Islam. It is for the Muslim learned to stand up and draw the line whenever this principle is challenged in the future as they have so valiantly done in the past. This right to chop and change Islam's basic laws is not vested in anyone including the Muslim ruler.

2.2 The example of the greatest caliph of Islam, Umar ibn Al- Khattab (RA), given in his ten year rule in terms of piety, standard of justice and care, concern for the poor, courage and steadfastness is preserved for posterity and for all future rulers of Muslims. Muslims do not expect some present day rulers to get rid of their air-conditioned cars and air conditioned palaces, which Umar (RA) with much greater authority and power than them did not have and would not have cared to have. But Muslims do expect their rulers to show greater concern for the welfare of the *Ummah* and uphold Islamic values and ideals. Those who are unable to do so are unfit to rule.

3. Working example of an Islamic state.

The British belief that it takes years, perhaps a century for institutions or systems to develop and mature is a debatable point. Perhaps it is so in British type of institutional development. Umar (RA), however, proved that in ten years one can achieve with faith, determination and proper logistics what may take many more years without these qualities. He established almost from scratch a successful working model of an Islamic state while conquering two mighty empires - Byzantine and Persian. And he did not have computers, Think Tanks and specialist advisers, though he did have faith! It is possible for Muslims today to visibly change their situation in no more than ten to twenty years, with total transformation of their status in no more than twenty-five to thirty years, if they go the right way about it and if they have faith.

There are of course many other lessons to be learnt by a detailed study of the life of the rightly guided caliphs. They ruled as follows:

Abu-Bakr as-Siddiq (RA)   632 AD - 634 AD

Umar ibn al-Khattab (RA)   634 AD - 644 AD

Uthman ibn Affan (RA)   644 AD - 656 AD

Ali ibn Abi Talib (RA)   656 AD - 661 AD

They ruled well and they ruled justly. It is a sad reflection on some of their successors today that they are neither ruling well nor justly.

Islamic State/Political System

There is much talk these days about the Islamic State, Islamic government and Islamic political system among Muslims and non-Muslims. Western journalists and writers some of whom have not made any serious effort in understanding the principles and purposes of such a state label it as Islamic fundamentalism, terrorism etc. To them there are only three forms of government; Western democracy, the communist or socialist system and dictatorship. They do not realise or perhaps do not want to admit that there is a fourth system of government which has been tried and tested and has proved itself a more superior system compared to the other three.

Why is it superior to all the other systems? Why it has not yet been implemented in more Muslim countries? What are its future prospects?
We discuss briefly the issues here which hopefully will provide some answers.

The Islamic system of government is a theocracy. It has a clearly defined and firm basis for the government of the state. There must be leadership. Government must be just and must provide for and look after the weak. It must be conducted on a two way channel of rectification - the leadership consulting the citizens and the citizens constructively criticising the leadership. Both the governed and the governing must mobilise their individual and collective powers to fight evil within themselves and to defend the faith. The government must abide by the rules of penalties, retaliation, justice, *halal* and *haram*. The distinguishing mark of an Islamic State is the clear definition of its accountability. Democracy itself is a broad based concept in an Islamic State with both greater degree of responsibility and accountability.

The accountability is dual; the head of a State and its ministers and officials are accountable to Allah (SWT) the Ultimate Sovereign and also to the citizens of the state. In the Islamic system religion has not been divorced from the government as in the West. Religion is part of the government and the government is an extension of religion. It is this aspect of governance in a Muslim majority country that upsets the secular West because of their deep belief that religion and politics are two separate issues. Islam says and good Muslims believe that they are one and the same. In fact we would go so far as to make a provocative statement that it would be impossible to govern morally, justly and absolutely fairly in any system of government other than the Islamic system. We challenge anyone to prove us wrong!

Source of Ultimate Power - Basis of Government.

In an Islamic state the source of all power and the depository of sovereignty of the state is in Allah (SWT). All basic and fundamental laws as laid down by Allah (SWT) for the conduct of government must be followed. Human beings have a right to make detailed legislation and exercise the authority to govern and administer but it must be within the boundaries of the laws of Allah (SWT). This right is exercised by the head of the state and his ministers on the principle that man is vicegerent of Allah on earth. Vicegerent means a person exercising delegated power, in this case power delegated by Allah (SWT). The extent and details of this power and authority are The Qur'an (Allah's Book) and *sunnah* (Allah's Messenger's deeds, sayings and examples). The cumulative body of Islamic laws by which the country is governed is known as *shari'ah*. Allah's believing citizens, through their nominated/elected representatives in the *Shura* and other institutions of the Islamic State are His watchdogs.

Some cynics might say what Allah (SWT) has got to do with governments and why should He be looked upon as a Sovereign instead of HM the Queen, Prime minister Major or indeed President Clinton? The answer to this perplexing inquiry is simple. In fact there are two answers to this question. If you had a clear choice where you were to be ruled absolutely by the laws created by and authority exercised by the Queen, Major and Clinton on one hand or Allah (SWT) or God on the other whom will you choose? Even non-practising Muslims and Christians will choose Allah (SWT) or God to Clinton and Major. As for the Queen she might get some royalists on her side but not many. This choice of being governed by Allah's (SWT) laws is decidedly a better one for any who believes in the Creator, compared to being governed by the laws of mortal men. This choice is now only available from an Islamic system of government. Also the Islamic system is less likely to be misused than any other system.

It is a total system with total involvement and total accountability. There may be ifs and buts on the minor details but none on the basic principles which has been made crystal clear. Fortunately for Muslims, Allah's true believers do not require the approval of Congress or the Houses of Parliament to OK this System. The System was OK long before the 'Congress' and 'HOP' existed and will be OK in future.

Shurah: Consultation.
Majlis-e-Shura: Consultative assembly whose members may be elected or appointed. It is an essential institution in Islamic governance and social/legislative matters. It is not a sovereign body like some parliaments in some secular countries.
Shari'ah: Islamic law based on the Qur'an, hadith, ijma and qiyas.

Islamic Governance Vs Western type of Democracy.
The Islamic government although more democratic than the Western democracies in concept is the very anti-thesis of it. The principal difference is that in the Western democracy the ultimate power to make laws is vested in the people through their elected representatives. Good or bad laws can be made and put on the statute book if the people so choose. Also basic laws can get changed with the change in attitude. Hanging has been allowed at some time or other in some countries. It is allowed in some states in USA while in others it is not, although the states are part of one sovereign country. Both laws cannot be right. Some member countries of the United Nations ban homosexuality while others fully recognise and allow it backed by legislation. Questions of morality do not come into it.

Recently a new entrant has penetrated into the citadel of democracy. It is the lobbyists. They are already a powerful force in the United States, Japan and France and a growing force in other democracies. It can be said that powerful lobbying of special interests can result in corrupting and unjust laws. Even diehard secularists now think that there is something wrong with the system of democracy and perhaps this should be changed to a more representative and referendum type of democracy. This is simply jumping from one frying pan to another. With the decline in morality, increase in racial prejudice and growing strength of special interests there is no guarantee that greater people power will result in either better government or better laws. In fact it is bad news for the minority citizens of any country. Such grouping of majority citizens may pass laws totally against the interests of its minority fellow citizens even depriving them of their basic rights.

Ijtehad: Exertion. A logical deduction of a learned man of Islam. It is one of the major sources of Islamic jurisprudence.

Accountability of an Islamic State.

The Islamic State is accountable to Allah (SWT) both collectively and individually. All those who have authority have this accountability, from the head of the government to the lowest official. This is to ensure that only proper and just laws based on Qur'an, sunnah and *ijtehad* are made, implemented and applied with justice, wisdom, fairness and due compassion in accordance with the *shari'ah*. The making of detailed laws is not enough - the proper application of those laws is of greater importance. Divine laws give unconditional guarantee of fairness, justice, equality, welfare and safety of property and person even to the lowliest citizens of the Islamic state. No lobbyist or majority party can deprive them of these rights. If these laws are not applied in practice in accordance with Divine Commandment in a country then its government cannot be termed an Islamic government. A prime example of this is Pakistan. It is not an Islamic state at present but a very corrupt halfway house.

Purpose of the Islamic State.

Here the Islamic system differs widely from all other systems of government. Governments everywhere have become an arena of political and economic power to be grabbed by one group and imposed, during the term of the office, on the rest of the groups. It is also a reflection of the country's power and weight in the international field through their governments for manipulative and destructive politics irrespective of the consequences to ordinary people both at home and abroad. Exploitation of the resources of the poorer countries to meet the needs, expectations and standard of living of the richer countries is done in the name of democracy and their elected representatives. Almost any thing goes in the name of 'our National Interest', without much concern for morality or adverse consequences to third parties. In some types of governments such as communism or dictatorship the situation is much worse.

In the case of an Islamic State any such exploitation will not be permitted. There is no special privilege to any particular class of people, tribe or group. Heads of state and government officials are there not to exploit the resources of the country or enjoy special privileges but to serve in the true sense of the word. It is deemed to be a government of the people to serve the people in accordance with Allah's (SWT) Commands. Principles of morality will have an important bearing on the Islamic state particularly in relation to its dealings with third parties.

The basis of legislation of an Islamic State.

The basis of legislation of an Islamic State is Qur'an and *sunnah*. The manner of its adoption and implementation is through the medium of consultation by the process of *shura* which means to take decision by consultation and participation. The Council of *shura* or a special committee from it can be used to decide on such laws and matters for which the Qur'an and *sunnah* have not laid down detailed rules. Governments, particularly in modern age, are complex organisations and there will be some situations where new laws, rules or procedures need to be made and implemented. This is done by the process of *ijma* and *qiyas* within the broad principles laid down in the Qur'an and *sunnah*. *Ijma* means consensus of the Muslim community, normally

---

Ijma: Collecting or assembling. Unanimous consent of the learned men of Islam. It is a source of Islamic jurisprudence.

Qiyas: To compare. Another pillar of Islamic jurisprudence in which logical reasoning is used by the learned of Islam to teach, explain and resolve religious and other issues.

Raai: Individual reasoning in general is called *raai* or opinion.

Istehsan: Where there is more than one view on a point and only one view is to be preferred on account of its appropriateness in accordance with Qur'an and Sunnah, such process of exercising preference is called *istehsan*.

represented by its learned. *Qiyas* means the process of thought, reasoning, thinking and deliberation. *Qiyas* can take the form of *Ijtehad, Istehsan* and *Raai.*

Head of the State of an Islamic State and its organisational structure.

There are no detailed organisational charts or titles provided by Qur'an and *sunnah* for an Islamic State. There is consensus, however, that the head of an Islamic State should be called a caliph. The head of an Islamic state can be a Caliph, President, Sultan, Emir, King or Prime-Minister. It is not the title but the quality of his leadership that is important. Similarly the detailed organisational structure for the running of the government, its economy, its armed and foreign services, its social and welfare services may vary from one Muslim country to another depending on many local circumstances. The type of organisational structure can be decided by the elected representatives of the people and as long as they do not exceed the bounds of *shari'ah* i.e. the basic law as given by the Qur'an and *sunnah*, the structural details can have variations.

Some Muslims think that we should have one caliph for all the Muslims throughout the world. This is indeed the ideal objective but with sixty Muslim countries it is not a practical and achievable task in the immediate future. The most appropriate way forward for majority of Muslim countries is to become well managed, just, and technically, educationally advanced Islamic states individually or in regional groupings. The next step should be for them to unite under Islamic organisations such as a 'Muslim United Nations' and 'Muslim Security Council'. Such a forum is essential for mutual consultation, help and defence and also to represent any special case or any special interest of Muslims to the main world body that is the United Nations or the Security Council. At present Muslim states influence on world affairs is next to nought and this is only because of lack of unity and their backwardness.

Independent Judiciary and Equality of all before Law in an Islamic State.

Justice and equality are the cardinal principles of an Islamic State. This can best be explained by an example. In the United Kingdom Queen Elizabeth II as the sovereign is above law and exempt from it. The head of an Islamic State and all government officials are equal in law to ordinary citizens and anyone can be asked to come to the courts if necessary. Islamic justice recognises no basis for discrimination, and grants no exemptions to anyone. Even non-Muslims have protection under the law for their life, belief, property and honour. Preference and any notion of superiority in Islam for one compared to another is based on the degree of piety -*taqwa*- of the former over the latter.

Economics & Banking, Welfare and Morality control Systems in an Islamic State.

The fundamental rules here are the absence of interest -*riba* - and the payment of the religious tax -*zakah*. Welfare of the poor, sick and the needy has the first claim on the resources of the Islamic State. Laws to protect morality particularly social and public morality are the next important items.

Conclusion.

Western democracy as it is being practised today in the West is a cruel joke. We do not wish to insult the intelligence of our readers by pointing to the recent example of Italy and Japan. Here the system has not just been abused but reached its nadir in corruption. Democracy, at its cradle here in Europe is allowing the wholesale slaughter of innocent people in the Balkans. Knowledgeable Muslims believe that

Western democracy is as unsuitable for Muslim countries, as an absolute dictatorship is unsuitable for UK. Because of the very special nature of an Islamic state it can never be brought into existence by armed revolution alone. The establishment of an Islamic state in its true sense requires grassroots work among the Muslims of the country. The Muslims must be sufficiently just, obedient to Allah (SWT) and must have not only faith but also practice that faith in their daily lives. Only then they will be able from among them to choose just and pious leaders whether prince or pauper. A *hadith* related to the Prophet (SAAS) confirms that,

'A people get the ruler, they deserve.'

Corrupt people cannot have a just ruler and just people cannot put up with a corrupt ruler for long.

The true *jihad* for our young, for our intellectuals and for our learned is to do grassroots work among the people with the true message of Islam, both in Muslim majority and Muslim minority countries. This is the seed that must be planted, germinated and nourished to grow strong in a Muslim society. All else will follow in proper order from this seed - the tree, the branches, the fruit, the protection of the shade and the power of the blade. The article on Mosque explains how this revival can be achieved.

Islam's history shows that Islamic states of the past had been both very tolerant and accommodating of people of other faiths. The Jews were a persecuted people before Muslim rule in Spain. For seven hundred years during Muslim rule they enjoyed peace, security and religious freedom. This was followed by their equally good treatment

---

Jihad: Means striving in the way of Allah (SWT) with personal effort, material resources or arms on the side of righteousness but against tyranny and oppression. *Jihad* is also armed struggle in the defence of Muslim community.

under the Ottoman Caliphate. A large number of Jews still live in Turkey. There is no example in history of such tolerance.

Summary.

The essence of an Islamic state can be summed up in just one sentence. It is to forbid evil and promote virtue and govern with the highest possible standards of justice, equality, care and concern within incorruptible Divine rules and with accountability to Allah (SWT) and the people. It is not an Utopian system but a system which was tried and tested over centuries. This system is more suitable and appropriate now than ever before. In fact its suitability and need grows in direct proportion to our advancement in science and technology. This is because it is the only system that balances morality with immorality, humility with big-headedness, justice with injustice and exploitation, the negative with the positive. The following two verses from the Qur'an are samples of this governance. There are other verses and numerous *hadith* on this subject.

"...And government is by counsel among themselves..."
(Surah Shura 42:38)

"O you who believe! Be maintainers of justice, bearer of witness for Allah's sake though it may be against your own selves, parents and relatives and whether it be against rich or poor..."
(Surah Nisaa 4:135)

We posed three questions on the Islamic state at the beginning of this article. We should be able to answer them now.

Why the Islamic system of government is superior to all other systems?

The comparison is really between democratic system as in the West vs Islamic system. The democratic system is the representative system. In between elections which can last from four to seven years our chosen representatives can do almost anything. Sometimes it is even difficult to distinguish whether our representatives are acting properly or improperly. There are no strict moral codes to guide legislation affecting individuals conduct in society, children or women for example. With suitable lobbying laws can be passed and have been passed legalising prostitution, homosexuality, lesbianism, drug taking, abortion. There is no stopping this moral depravity. Perversity of the worst order is now shown in public on television, newspapers, books and magazines in areas which were once left in the private domain. They are having a deadly effect on the younger generation. All this because moral safeguard of religion has been thrown out of the window of secularism with man assuming himself to be smarter than Allah (SWT) in conducting his affairs all by himself. Many rulers have proved themselves either complete dodos or tyrant maniacs under other systems and the leaders in the democratic system have provided their voters a free ride on the immorality and exploitation gravy train. The Islamic system has a built in safeguard against such possibilities.

Why it has not yet been implemented in more Muslim countries?

In our opinion because of the following reasons:

a. Although all Muslim countries are now independent this independence has only come to them in the last fifty years after nearly hundred to three hundred years of colonial and communist rule. Under their secularised colonial rulers many Muslim intellectuals were so mesmerised with the Western system and became such intellectual softies that even now they hanker after Western democracy when the West itself is questioning the effectiveness of its own system. Only recently serious re-thinking has commenced in few Muslim countries as to whether we should go Islamic or not despite the fact that there is no better system.

b. After independence or the creation of many nation-states power was deliberately handed over to some Western toadies. In other cases it was grabbed under all sorts of false pretences by the opportunist leaders. Once grabbed they are staying put under non-Islamic or artificial Islamic systems. To many of these rulers a true Islamic government means loss of power and privilege and the disappearance of their swiss bank accounts. Naturally they are hanging on by fair means or foul.

c. In some cases an Islamic system of government has not come into existence because of the direct scheming of Western powers. The West thinks that an Islamic government is not in its best 'National Interests'. This is of course absurd because this is the only form of government that is in everybody's interest including the West. The only losers are the handful of toadies at the top in these Muslim majority countries. The West must reconsider its position and perhaps Western Think Tanks will re-examine the issue objectively and honestly.

What are its future prospects?

In one word - excellent. There are already some Islamic states on the scene and others are adopting Islamic ways. The peace in the Middle East will be the greatest spur to the demise of dictators. No longer they can exploit the masses in the name of pushing the Israelis to the sea. Muslims will not mind who rules them; a king, a sheikh, a caliph or a prime minister as long he rules justly in accordance with Islamic laws as given in the Qur'an and *sunnah*. Those rulers who cannot do so must take it for granted that their days are numbered. We live in an age of information explosion and a new armoury of persuasion in the computer, the fax machine and the ham radio is now available. No unjust ruler can survive long once a *jihad* is declared against him using the true powers of the computer, the fax machine, the ham radio, the audio and video cassette and of course the printed word. So the prospects of many more true Islamic states are very encouraging and this must be good news for the West.

The flow chart shows approximate outline of an ideal Islamic State.

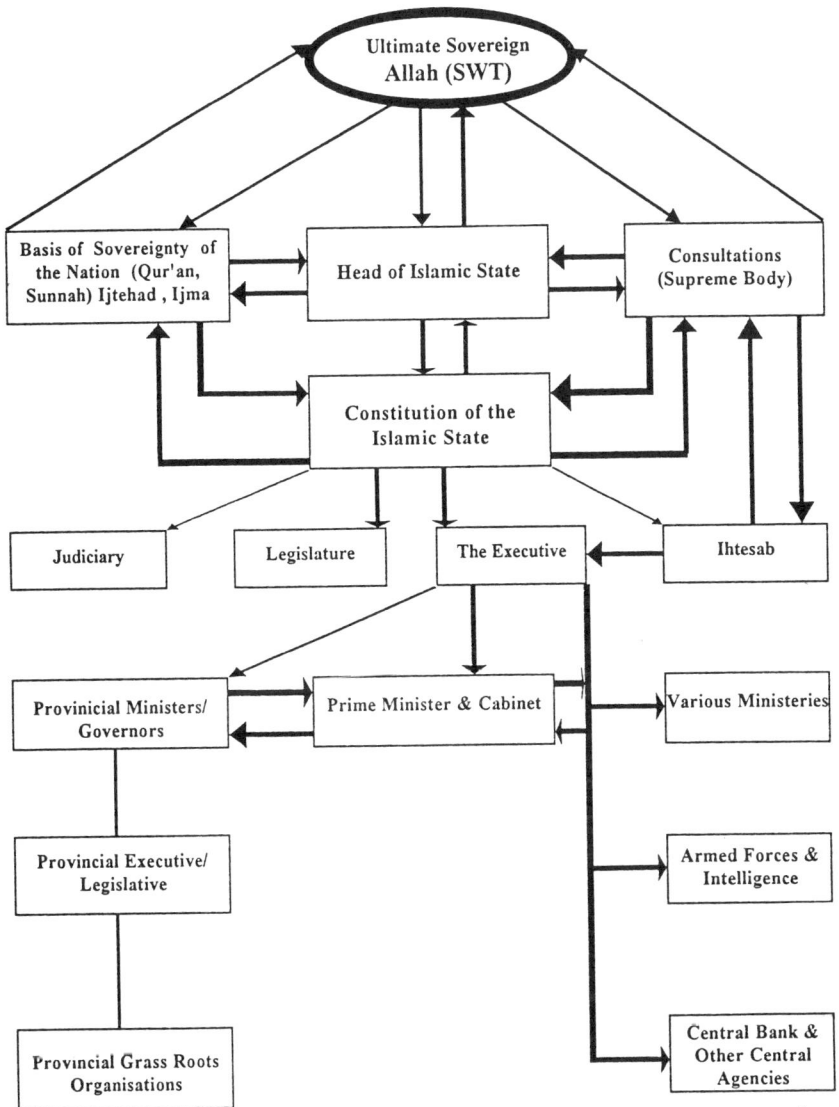

Outline Structure of an Islamic State

The Learned and Islam

The learned in Islam have always played an important role. Such early thinkers as al-Ghazzali, Ibn-Taymiyya and Sheikh Ahmad Sirhindi have left us a vast legacy of literature, wisdom, ideas and methodology about Islam's on-going revival and renaissance. A great deal of contribution to the Islamic renaissance has been made by Muslim scholars of the recent past. Among this group can be included such notable names as Shah Wali-ullah, Syed Ahmed Khan, Ibn Abd al-Wahab, Uthman Dan Fodio, Muhammad Ali ibn al-Sanussi, Sir Muhammad Iqbal, Jamaluddin Afghani, Md. Abduh, Rashid Ridah, Hassan al-Banna, Md. Qutb and Maulana Maududi. This list is by no means exhaustive. Some of the present Muslim thinkers and writers are in a different mould to these scholars. They have the benefit of not only a sound religious education but have been able to combine it with advanced secular education and degrees (a desirable development which is likely to continue). One can safely say at this point of time that there is now a good deal of consensus among Muslim thinkers and the silent majority of the *Ummah* on such important issues as the urgent desirability of setting up Islamic states in Muslim countries, the urgent need to develop Muslim countries to the same advanced level as many Western countries, the urgent need for Muslims every where to improve the quality of their faith and its practice and to maintain and project high standards of Islamic moral values, conduct and identity. A consensus is also gradually developing as to how to go about attaining these objectives.

Two groups of Muslims feel threatened by this new development. The first group is made up of the dictators and the tyrants who have usurped power in some Muslim countries. They see their inevitable demise in the Islamic revival. To them only one advice need be given; change immediately for the better for Islam or in the name of Allah (SWT) Go! The other group is made up of some of the die-hard traditionalist Muslim learned and not so learned. To some of them the earth is still flat. Some in this group often do not have the benefit of a sound general education. Their understanding of the word *Ilm* and development is at odds with its true meaning. The word *Ilm* has been taken in the past by them to mean religious or revealed knowledge only and *Alim* or plural *Ulama*, all those who have this knowledge. This restricted and narrow interpretation of knowledge has done immense harm to Muslims. All knowledge belongs to Allah (SWT) and therefore any one is an *Alim* who has knowledge revealed or otherwise. There should not be the slightest doubt or disagreement among Muslims that in Islam the most valuable and essential knowledge that must be acquired first is revealed knowledge. We would go so far as to say that the acquisition of any other knowledge by a Muslim, however valuable, before he has acquired the minimum revealed knowledge of the Qur'an and some knowledge of the *sunnah* is an unworthy and unacceptable achievement. However, the acquisition of revealed knowledge is not the end of acquiring knowledge. It is the beginning.

The twenty-first century *Alim* in Islam will be a person who is well versed in both revealed and other knowledge. No one who is only well versed in revealed knowledge can of be of great use to the *Ummah*. Muslims must appeal to all these traditional scholars that they urgently overhaul their *Madrasahs* and other establishments and institutions to cater for Islam's future needs. They have made great sacrifices of

---

Ilm: The knowledge includes religious knowledge first followed by other knowledge. Also learning, information, perception.

Ulama: Scholars, learned men, knowledgable men. Generally referred to religious scholars of Islam.

their lives and liberties in the past in defending and serving Islam. The Islamic revival and the grassroots work required for it needs them more than ever before but it needs them better educated and better trained than at any time in the past.

Another important issue of the so called learned that we must address is their exploitation by some corrupt governments. This is being done either by money or privilege or a combination of both. In this area some of the so called learned of Islam have caused great damage to it by associating themselves with secular rulers like the late Nasser in the past. And despite defeats, economic and social disorders brought by these rulers there are still some so called learned Muslims who are allowing themselves to be used by them knowing full well that these rulers are neither following Islam nor ruling according to its teachings. Some of the learned are also causing regular embarrassment by in-fighting among themselves on insignificant issues. **The future should now be crystal clear to our learned. It is now pristine Islam with its traditional moral, political, social, financial values that must march forward with modern science, technology and development.** Both are totally compatible. There will be some grey areas that would require further debate, deliberation and discussion. After all *Ijtehad* is a continuous process. It is here that the present and future learned of Islam must exert themselves at all levels of debate in a constructive and co-operative manner. They should step up propaganda and take all possible action that is within their power against manifestly unjust and un-Islamic rulers wherever they may be.

The future method of operation by the *Ulama* also needs overhaul. The changing role of the *Imam* in the local community, the importance of social and welfare work for

---

Ijtehad: Exertion. A logical deduction of a learned man of Islam.

dawah, the rising demand for the services of the *Ulama* in the newly emerging Muslim countries, and the need for them in countries where Muslims are in conflict or in danger require a speedier and more efficient response from our learned. The *Ulama*, the soldier and the relief worker must march forward together in many theatres of Muslim global activity backed by the scientist, technologist and the just leaders of Islam not for confrontation but for reconciliation and defence. The emphasis in future will be greater practical action and involvement in the affairs of Muslims than theorising. The learned of Islam have a very significant role to play at present and in future in all the affairs concerning the *Ummah*.

Islamic Banking, Trade and Investment

The central theme in Islamic banking, trade and investment is interest - *riba*. Islam allows trade but forbids interest in the strongest terms and aims at establishing an economy not only free from all forms of interest but also from what bears any resemblance to it. On the other hand the modern economy is based on interest to such an extent that it is difficult to visualise any set of economic relations where interest does not come in directly or indirectly. How to resolve this contradiction is a challenge that is confronting many Muslims and particularly those Muslim countries who have introduced interest free banking as a parallel system together with their existing banking systems.

Great deal of progress has been made in the last thirty years by Islamic bankers and economists in devising various systems, models and developing details on how to eliminate interest and evolve new institutions and practices which would enable economic activities to flourish without resort to interest - *riba* - in any form.

The basic system of Islamic trade and investment relies on *Musharika* which means active business partnership between investors and producers/traders on the basis of sharing profit and loss in pre-agreed ratios. Where manufactured goods are concerned the system is based on *istisna* which is a contract where the subject matter is combination of the service of manufacturing as well as the manufactured commodity for delivery at a future date. The contract is binding for both situations if it fulfils certain conditions.

There are numerous ways of lending, borrowing, leasing that have been successfully developed to cater for trade and investment in the prescribed Islamic manner.

In addition to the prohibition of - *riba* - there is another important prohibition in business and trading activity for Muslims i.e. bribery and trading or carrying out any business activity in any product or service which the *shari'ah* has declared as *haram*.

For example it is unlawful for a Muslim to engage in any trade selling alcohol or to own and operate a gambling joint, a dance studio, a modelling agency. Muslims have also been given clear instructions in the Qur'an and *hadith* to conduct their trade and commerce in an honest and honourable way.

"And when the prayer is finished, then may you disperse through the land, and seek Bounty of Allah (through trade, business and undertaking lawful profession): and celebrate the praises of Allah that you may prosper."
(Surah Jumu'a 62:10)

"Woe to those that deal in fraud, those who, when they have to receive by measure from men exact full measure, but when they have to give by measure or weight to men, give less than due. Do they not think that they will be called to account? On a Mighty Day."
(Surah Al-Mutaffifin 83:1-5)

The following *ahadith* of Prophet Muhammad (SAAS) is noteworthy:

'A trustworthy and an honest and truthful businessman will rise up with martyrs on the day of Resurrection.' (Tirmidhi)

'Blessings of Allah be on him who is mild and gentle in his business transactions and in the realisation of his dues.' (Muslim)

Basically the entire Islamic system of trade, finance banking and investment is based on prohibition of interest. There is a great deal of Divine wisdom behind it which is even more relevant today than ever before. Individuals, businesses, families and whole societies and countries are affected by the evils of unrestricted credit and interest which has caused and is causing enormous misery due to greed, irresponsible conduct and lack of morality in the financial transaction. The Islamic wisdom of prohibiting interest can be summarised as follows:

The wisdom of Prohibiting Interest.

The strict prohibition of interest in Islam is a result of its deep concern for the moral, social, and economic welfare of mankind. Islamic scholars have given sound arguments explaining the wisdom of this prohibition, and recent studies and global debt problems have confirmed their opinions.

1. The taking of interest implies appropriating another person's property without giving him anything in exchange, because one who lends one dollar for two dollars gets the extra dollar for nothing. Now, a man's property is for (the purpose of) fulfilling his needs and it has great sanctity, according to the *hadith*, 'A man's property is as sacred as his blood.' This means that taking it from him without giving him something equivalent in exchange is *haram*.

2. Dependence on interest prevents some people with capital from working to earn money, since the person with dollars can earn extra dollars through interest, either in advance or at a later date, without working for it. The value of work ethic will consequently be reduced in his estimation, and he may not bother to take the trouble of running a business or risking his money in trade or industry. This may lead to depriving people of benefits, since further and fuller employment is only possible where there is industrial and commercial activity. One of the great fears that some major investors have these days is the prospect of interest rising in the near future. If they have capital they are often reluctant to invest in productive businesses because they hope to earn more by lending the capital on high rates of interest. If they don't have capital they are reluctant to borrow for fear of making high interest payments. Either way productive investment loses out. The large scale speculation by holders of capital in moving their money where it will earn higher rates of interest has cost billions to governments and the tax payers, for the benefit of few lenders. This, from an economic point of view, is unquestionably a weighty argument.

3. Permitting the taking of interest discourages people from doing good to one another, as is required by Islam. If interest is prohibited in a society, people will lend to each other with good will, expecting back no more than what they have loaned for a share of agreed profits, while if interest is made permissible the needy person will be required to pay back more on loans (than he has borrowed) thus weakening his feelings of goodwill and friendliness toward the lender. This is the moral aspect of the prohibition of interest.

4. The lender is very likely to be wealthy and the borrower poor. If interest is allowed, the rich will exploit the poor, and this is against the spirit of mercy and charity. This is the social aspect of the prohibition of interest.

Thus, in a society in which interest is lawful, the strong benefit from the suffering of the weak. As a result, the rich become richer and the poor poorer, creating socio-economic classes in the society separated by wide gulfs. This generates envy and hatred among the poor toward the rich, and contempt and callousness among the rich toward the poor. It gives rise to conflict, the socio-economic fabric is torn apart, revolutions are born, and social order and justice is threatened. Recent history amply illustrates the dangers to the peace and stability of nations inherent in interest based economies.

A hadith says:

'Allah has cursed the one who takes interest, the one who pays it, the one who writes the contract, and the one who witnesses the contract.' (Bukhari and Muslim)

One of the greatest scourge of interest has resulted in two continents - Africa and South America - virtually brought down on their knees with the burden of debt. They owe hundreds of billions of dollars to Western banks and a large portion of their national income is spent in paying interest on these loans. Africa, despite all this borrowing has nowhere improved either its environment or the economic health of its people. There is famine, inefficiency, corruption and moral decline in which credit, interest, greed for wealth and moral degeneration have played a leading part.

Muslim bankers and governments must accelerate the Islamic system of banking by further advanced research, opening up new faculties for undergraduate and post graduate studies. International conferences, seminars and interchange of ideas should take place on ever greater scale. Muslim businessmen should be encouraged by Islamic governments to utilise Islamic banking and Muslim investors should invest in Islamic banks a portion of their savings.

Islam and Science

For many Muslims it is often a matter of some concern and shock why there are so few great scientists among them - practically none in Arab countries. They also wonder why Muslim contribution to advanced science and technology is so meagre. This state of affairs has given an ammunition to some non-Muslims to attack Islam as a non-scientific religion. They also propagate that Islam does not encourage the pursuit of knowledge and acquisition of scientific disciplines.   While the concern and wonder expressed by Muslims are true the conclusions drawn from this state of affairs is not correct.

The Qur'an encourages the acquisition of knowledge - all knowledge. And Prophet Muhammad (SAAS), whose life was 'Living Islam' stimulated the desire for knowledge, travel and the spreading of Islam's message among Arabs in such a way and to such an extent that in a few decades they became the masters of all the Sciences of their time. This is a well known and acknowledged fact. There is no denying the fact that Muhammad's (SAAS) teachings were later responsible for the Renaissance in Europe. The Arabs of Spain were the chief source of the new learning and scientific spirit of the Europeans. There is also no doubt that the seeds from Arabic science first germinated in the seed beds of the schools of Lorraine in Latin Europe. From there knowledge radiated to other parts of Europe and to the English Universities of Oxford and Cambridge. French and German Universities were also established on the pattern of the Muslim universities of Spain and Baghdad.

The glory of Muslim Science in all its aspects in the fields of geography, astronomy, astrology, physics, chemistry, mathematics, optics, history, medicine, natural history and many other fields of learning has left its permanent mark on the sciences of modern Europe. And it is now fully documented in many texts and history books.

The Muslim scientists such as Al-Biruni, Ibn Rushd, Al-Battani, Abu Ma'shar, Al-Farqhani, Al-Khwarizmi, Al-Kindi, Al-Razi and literally hundreds others have left their mark on history. Unfortunately a great deal of Muslim literary and scientific treasures were deliberately and systematically destroyed. This happened first in Baghdad after the Mongol invasion in the thirteenth century when practically all the libraries were burnt and the scholars slaughtered. In the fifteenth century after the fall of Muslim Spain to the Catholics a greater destruction of the Muslim heritage of science and literature was carried out. Many later scientists and thinkers deliberately not gave any credit to Muslim scientific sources from where they borrowed. It is this reason why we hear so little about Muslim contribution to science in the West.

The West owes much to Islam for the Muslim's early contribution and development in the intellectual and scientific fields. In these areas, borrowed words tell some of the story; algebra, cipher, zero, nadir, amalgam, alembic, alchemy, alkali, soda, almanac, and names of many stars such as Aldebran and Betelgeuse. Islamic civilisation both preserved and expanded Greek philosophical and scientific knowledge when such knowledge was almost entirely forgotten in the West. All the important Greek scientific works surviving from ancient times were translated into Arabic and most of these in turn were translated in the medieval West from Arabic into Latin. Above all, the preservation and interpretation of the works of Aristotle was one of Islam's most enduring accomplishments. Not only was Aristotle first re-acquired in the West by means of the Arabic translations, but he was interpreted with Islamic help, above all that of Averroes, whose prestige was so great that he was simply called 'the Commentator' by medieval Western writers. Arabic numerals, too, rank as a tremendously important intellectual legacy from Islam.

It is a matter of regret that with such a rich legacy from the past Muslims have presently fallen so far behind. One cannot even accuse Western Imperialism, a familiar catch phrase, since many Muslim countries have now been independent for nearly fifty years. Despite the growth of wealth, education, manpower and availability of abundant resources Muslim countries have not realised, encouraged or invested into advanced research areas both theoretical and applied. They have become totally dependent on outside technical and scientific aid and know how.

It is hoped that with the renewal and revival of Islam richer Muslim countries will realise the importance of setting up advanced research and technological institutions, science parks and advanced manufacturing industries. If it is not accomplished urgently neither their security nor their stability is guaranteed for the future. There is no substitute for indigenous knowledge. Scientific and technical knowledge and know-how should be of special interest to Islam and Muslims. This is because technical and scientific competence enables a nation to serve their own people better, as well as others outside their country. Knowledge and know-how in Islam are for the purpose of serving Allah's (SWT) creation; it is neither to dominate others nor threaten them. Knowledge and know-how give any country that has it a greater sense of security and well being. **The modern model of a truly civilised country and society is advanced knowledge and know-how combined with high standards of morality and piety. Islam encourages only this kind of model society.**

A tiny country like Israel does not now feel at all threatened by anyone including the larger and numerous Arab

States surrounding it. This is because it has both a free and representative government as well as scientific and technical know-how in all branches of science and technology at a very advanced level. And this knowledge is totally indigenous. It rightly gives Israelis the feeling of overwhelming superiority over its neighbours, to such an extent that even their national leaders have made derogatory statements to the effect that Arabs are stupid. The achievements of the Jewish state in a period of less than fifty years is remarkable indeed even allowing for the fact they had certain intellectual and educational advantages. Much larger countries than Israel like Saudi Arabia, Egypt, Pakistan are under constant security and stability threat because despite vast wealth (Saudi Arabia) and large populations (Egypt, Pakistan) they are in the backwoods of scientific and technical knowledge. They are perennially dependent on outsiders for technical and security support.

Muslim countries, particularly richer countries must realise and act as a matter of urgency to implement policies that promote advanced scientific, technical and management research in their own countries. Individual Muslims in East or West must recognise its importance and exert themselves in acquiring the highest possible qualifications and achieve academic and research excellence.

Muslims should feel pride in the fact that the Qur'an itself is a reservoir of basic scientific facts and scientific trends. The concept of 'Atom', 'birth', 'earth's roundness', 'orbiting of sun and moon and the planets', birth of all living creatures in pairs are mentioned in the Qur'an. Only recently many of these verses have been fully understood because to understand them fully, required scholarship of both classical Arabic language as well as scientific knowledge and the knowledge of latest scientific discoveries.

Any one who suggests that acquisition of advanced scientific and technical knowledge by Muslims is non-

Islamic belongs to the *Jahilliya* period. It is also foolish to suggest that the acquisition of such knowledge may affect one from being a good Muslim. On the contrary the better and more practising Muslims in future are likely to be those who are well versed in religious knowledge as well as have advanced scientific and technical qualifications. This is abundantly clear in the corridors of the citadels of learning and the research institutes where the new generation of Muslims learn and work. They are contributing to their personal development, to the development and better understanding of Islam and above all to the development and welfare of their adopted countries in the West. Except two Muslim countries no serious research is being undertaken at advanced level anywhere in the remaining fifty seven or so Muslim countries. Their research efforts and facilities are at the kindergarten level and their present contribution to science is almost nil.

Islamic Art and Literature

The population of the Middle East and elsewhere that adopted the Islamic faith from the 7th century onwards created an immense variety of literature, visual arts, performing arts, music. Islamic Art is divided into two parts - one arising directly from the practice of Islam, the other part is that produced by those newly converted Muslims who brought to Islamic art the influence of the arts, learning and heritage from their previous religion and culture. This latter part also covers arts produced in Pre-Islamic times by Arabs and others in Asia minor and North Africa who eventually adopted the Islamic faith and influenced it with their traditional art and craft on an on-going basis..

Islam does not allow representation of living beings as an expression of 'art'. The centre of Islamic artistic tradition lies in calligraphy which is a distinguishing feature of Islamic culture. In calligraphy the word as the medium of Divine revelation plays a very important part. The typical expression of Muslim art is the arabesque, both in its geometric and in its vegetaabolic form - one leaf, one flower growing out of the other, without a beginning or an end and capable of innumerable forms. One is able to detect its infinite charm gradually. This art is distinguished by its aversion to empty spaces; neither the tile covered walls of a mosque nor the rich inscription of Qur'anic verses allow an unblemished area - the decoration of a carpet can be extended endlessly without limit.

Europe has known art objects of Islamic origin since the early middle ages, when they were brought home by the Crusaders or manufactured by the Arabs and local artisans in Spain and Sicily. Such art objects were much admired and even imitated. They formed part of the material culture in those times, so much so that even the coronation robes of a

German emperor were decorated with Arabic inscription. At the same time Islamic motives wandered into the salons of Europe. Miniatures from Muslim India inspired Rembrandt, Persian carpets were the most coveted gifts for prince and princesses.

The golden period of Islamic art and literature declined with the demise of Muslim Spain in 13th/14th centuries then rose again during the Mughal empire from 15th to 18th century and during the Ottoman empire from 14th to 18th century.

For the Islamic countries the 19th century marks the beginning of a new and rather sad epoch because many of the Muslim countries were colonised and secular influence and Western culture penetrated their art, literature and systems of government.

The modern period of Islamic Art and literature can be said to begin after the second world war. Currently much of Muslim art and literature is directed towards addressing the social problems of Muslims, governance and good government, economic condition, struggle against Western influence, revival of Islam in the masses. A pride in their heritage and past achievements and their confidence to recreate it in the future also plays a very important role in the current output of Art and literature. Muslims are now realising that they can combine the traditional values and morals of Islam not only in developing Art but also science, technology and management including Islamic form of banking as well as Islamic system of welfare and government. The settlement in Europe and America of a large community of well educated and strong in faith Muslims is a sign of things to come in all fields of human and religious endeavour including art and literature. These Muslims are bound to influence and have their impact gradually felt in many areas of literature, science, art but particularly in areas of social and moral values and practice.

Muslim Contribution to Architecture, Mathematics and Morality

Constant gloating over one's past is not a good thing. It is the present and the future that matter. But any people who had a glorious past and who are at the bottom of the heap now must look to the past both nostalgically and as a means of deriving lessons to improve themselves for the present and the future.

There are still some persons both Muslims and non-Muslims who believe that pristine Islam of the Prophet (SAAS) and his companion's time is not conducive to modern achievements. They also think that some form of modernity must be introduced to Islam.

There are others who believe that Western ways of doing things such as the way of the democratic government and Western approach to things, such as divorcing religion (and of course morals with it) and politics in conducting the affairs of men are the best policy.

Islam is just Islam. It is neither old nor new; it is neither old fashioned nor modern. While its basic laws and rules which form the core rules have been and will always be same, in its details it is and will always be evolutionary and revolutionary. It is clear for anyone to see what the Western way of doing things and Western way of thinking has done to man's spiritual, physical and family environment. Family life is broken; environment is being damaged; spiritual and moral standards are at their lowest ebb, poverty and depravity have overtaken the continents of Africa, South America and many other regions of the world.

Such deterioration is the direct result of our ignoring the basic Islamic advice contained in just one sentence:

'The best path is the straight and middle path without any extremes.' This governs and should govern the Muslim approach in all areas of his conduct and endeavour. If one reflects one will soon come to the conclusion how and where this sound advice has been ignored and what has been the terrible consequences of ignoring it.

For material progress to be useful and meaningful a balance must be maintained with it in relation to ecological, environmental, moral and spiritual restraints and rules. Islamic achievements of the past maintained this balance. The contribution of West to art, architecture, science and technology has been significant but at the expense of ecology, environment and moral decline with far reaching consequences.

Below is a brief description of Muslim contribution to Architecture, Mathematics and Morality.

Architecture.

Church and other religious buildings in Europe owe a great deal to early Muslim architecture. The point arch which is a feature of the Western Gothic art was first built at the Ummayad mosque of Damascus and Qusayr Amrah. The horse shoe shape of the arches of this mosque was known in the West as Moorish arch and it subsequently became the Spanish National style. In addition the Spanish language has preserved many architectural terms of an Arabic origin which attest to its influence by Islamic architecture.

The architectural designs used for building the mosques in Cairo, Cordoba, Istanbul, Isfahan, and the Alhambra of Granada influenced European architecture a great deal. A system of vaulting based on intersecting arches and interacting ribs for structural support was first developed by Muslim architects for building large mosques, educational buildings and palaces. This system of vaulting enabled large spaces to be covered by a roof without the need for too many column supports with balance and elegance. Many of the ideas of fortification and battlements developed by the Saracens were copied by the crusaders. Outstanding example of ornamental battlement are to be found in the Tullun mosque in Cairo built in the ninth century.

The Taj Mahal in India, the Dome of the Rock in Jerusalem, and the Alhambra palace in Granada are outstanding examples of Muslim architecture. Muslims loved and encouraged the building of water fountains and the planting of flowers, shrubs and trees around mosques and palaces. Examples of these can be found from Mughal India and Ottoman Turkey. This contribution was in harmony with ecology and environment.

Mathematics.

The earliest prolific Muslim writer and contributor on mathematics was Al-Khawrizmi from whose name the word algorithm signifying the Arabic numerals one to nine and zero are derived. It was from the writings of Al-Khawrizmi on algebra, astronomy and arithmetic that Europe received decimal notation. The zero was known to Arabs at least two hundred and fifty years before it came to the West. Cipher (*sifr*, empty) and algebra are evidence of the part played by the Muslim Arabs in the early stages of development of the science of mathematical calculations. Al-Khazini developed the idea of equilibrium and gravity. Al-Battani invented the trigonometrical functions and Abu 'l-Wafa is credited with the concept of tangents in trigonometry. Abu 'l-Wafa taught the quadrature of the parabola and volume of the paraboloid. Habash developed table of cotangents used to determine the altitude of the sun by a formula developed by al- Battani. Al-Farabi's work on music contain the germs of the ideas of logarithm used for notes in a stringed instrument which are connected by logarithmic law.

Abu'l Abbas ibn Banna produced some seventy books on all branches of mathematics.   Many branches of higher mathematics bear traces of Muslim genius and contribution.
A great deal of Muslim literature including valuable manuscripts and many Muslim libraries were destroyed and Muslim scholars murdered by Catholic Christians of Spain and Mongol plunderers of Baghdad.   We are fortunate to have some evidence left of their contribution and for new evidence that is surfacing all the time as a result of painstaking research by both Muslim and non-Muslim scholars.

Morality.

Islam's greatest contribution to mankind is in the area of morality.   Islam does not recognise that religious, political, cultural and social life are separate entities. For a Muslim they interlink and are a integrated whole. It is this reason why moral and decent conduct as well as rules to safeguard them cannot be divorced from the day to day life of a Muslim. In Islam it is not possible to be a crook in daytime and a saint at night or to commit sin every week and attend the confessional on the weekend. As we have said before Muslim scientists, engineers, teachers, leaders and innovators are duty bound to pay due attention to moral precepts in all their work whether theoretical or applied. They are also duty bound by the injunctions of the Qur'an to take particular care against disturbing the natural laws of Allah (SWT), harming the environment, and making life difficult for other creations of Allah (SWT) such as animals and plants.

There is profound wisdom in these teachings of the Qur'an and *sunnah*. Had the West followed some of these Islamic principles we would not today be facing the ecological disaster on land, sea and air. In big cities it is difficult to breathe Allah's air for human beings, safe sanctuaries are getting scarcer for Allah's other creatures in our forests; food resources of the sea are being destroyed by over fishing and pollution. This is against the teachings and spirit of the Qur'an and *sunnah.* If the present destruction continues, the future for human beings looks bleak indeed.

The future.

We have mentioned elsewhere and we repeat that it is incumbent on every Muslim to acquire as much knowledge as possible. It is also expected from Muslim scientists, engineers, doctors, philosophers, scholars to make their contribution with the central aim of the welfare and well-being of the human race. They should exert their influence against waste of resources and destruction of environment.

Muslims individually and Muslim countries and governments must make every effort to develop science and technology so that Muslims can make individual as well as collective contributions on the above principles and not for the exploitation of man by man.

The following verses of the Qur'an are relevant to the theme of wastage:

"... eat and drink, but waste not by excess for Allah does not love the wasters."
(Surah Araaf 7:31)

"Those who, when they spend, neither give too lavishly nor yet hold back, and keep a happy medium"
(Surah Furqan 25:67)

Islam is the only religion that encourages acquisition of revealed knowledge as well as scientific knowledge by study, observation and experimentation. In this religion advanced science and technology are natural and Divinely approved partners with high standards of Muslim morality and piety. No other religion or system offers this unique combination.

Islam in Central Asia and Russia

One of the most important historical events of the 20th century is the sudden fall and disintegration of Marxism and Communism in the Soviet Union and in Eastern Europe. It is of immense importance to Muslims because in the former Soviet Union were annexed scores of Central Asian Muslim countries whose religion and natural resources were exploited for nearly 70 years by the Communists. They also suffered a great deal during the harsh Stalinist regime.

One Muslim country Kazakhstan alone is vast - bigger than the Indo Pakistan sub-continent, almost one-third of the United States and with vast natural resources. The flow chart shown here details autonomous Muslim republics in Central Asia and Muslim independent/majority states within the Russian Federation with some basic data. It should assist in a clearer understanding of the extent of Islam in this vast region.

In the past the Central Asian Region has produced numerous scholars of the Qur'an and *hadith*, men of letters, philosophers, scientists and artists who have contributed a great deal to the Islamic heritage.

The greatest and most well known of them is, of course, *Imam* Bukhari (RA), born in Bukhara (Uzbekistan) in 194 AH (810 CE) and buried near Samarqand (also in Uzbekistan).

Before they became Muslims the people of Central Asia followed many diverse religions - Christianity, Judaism, Buddhism etc. The first contact with the then Central Asian region of Khurasan/Mavernakhar by the Arabs was established either during the reign of Caliph Umar (RA) or Caliph Uthman (RA). Some writers claim a *hadith* related to the Prophet Muhammad (SAAS) himself predicting Islamisation of the Central Asian regions but we are unable to confirm it.

By the middle of the 7th Century, Arabs had settled in large numbers in central Asia particularly Khurasan and Mavernakhar. It was a Muslim general Qutaybah bin Muslim who conquered Bukhara, established a foothold and gradually converted its people to Islam. It was from this time onwards that Islam gradually spread into the vast Central Asian region which today borders Iran, Afghanistan, Turkey and Pakistan-four important Muslim countries.

The flexibility and simplicity of Islam attracted the peoples of Central Asia. Islam's ability to integrate diverse peoples, cultures and customs and its lack of complicated dogmas and its spiritual strength accelerated the spread of Islam in this region. As the process of Islamisation through ninth to eleventh centuries accelerated, numerous mosques and *madrasahs* were built. Bukhara, Samarqand, Mar, Urganch and many other cities became important learning and cultural centres of Islam. The produced many well known scholars, scientists , philosophers and artists.

For over 80 years this vast region was virtually closed during the communist rule of Soviet Union which recently collapsed. During this period Muslims in this region, in common with people of other faiths suffered great persecution, forced deportations and complete denial of religious freedom. Muslim children were forcibly fed on the diet of communism, religion was made taboo and any expression of faith was considered a crime against the state and mercilessly punished.

Despite such trauma in their history Islam never died in the Central Asian Republics and the flame was kept alight by the devoted few. With the sudden demise of the Communist rule and subsequent independence of many Islamic regions and States, Islam has revived in the area. But the entire region is temporarily bereft of total power and authority over its affairs despite recent independence. The shadow of Russia still looms large over them.

Old guard politicians, radical Muslims, moderate Muslims all want to play a role in the reconstruction of the various republics. We believe that the best can only be achieved by all concerned in following the middle course. They should try to establish just governments on the basis of Islamic principles. It is of vital importance for this region, which is endowed with vast natural resources to develop the various country's agriculture, industry, education and welfare systems and to set up institutions of higher learning and research. This alone can benefit the people in the region as well as in other parts of the world both Muslim and non-Muslim. The leaders of these countries will have miserably failed their people if all they did was to part with their natural resources to outsiders for a pittance.

The map below and the flowchart show Muslim countries of this region.

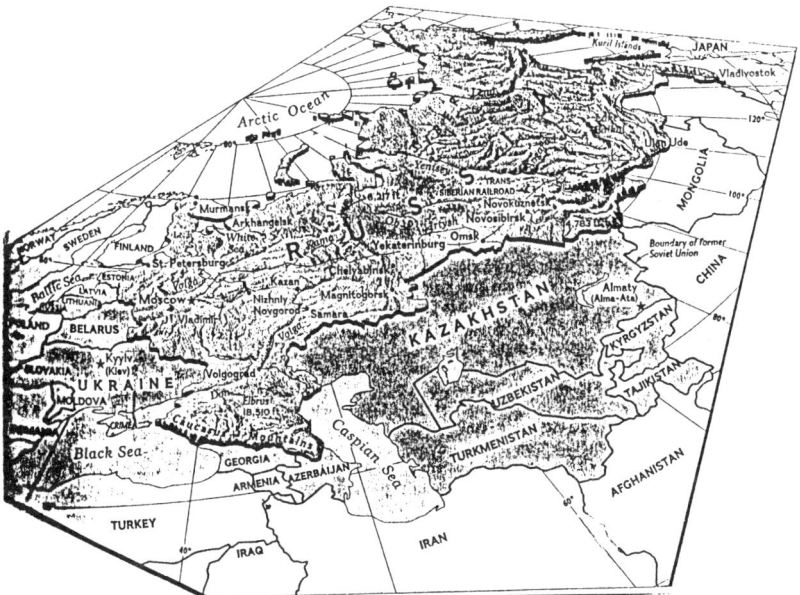

```
                    ┌─────────────────┐
                    │     Former      │
                    │ SOVIET REPUBLIC │
                    └─────────────────┘
```

	← Region →		← Region →		← Region →	
Central Asian		**Slavian**		**Transcau-casian**		**Prebaltic**

Uzbekistan	Area = 447,500 Sq. Km Total Pop. = 21,301,000 Muslim Pop. = 85%	**Moldovia**	**Armenia**

Lithuania

Tajikistan	Area =143,000 Sq. Km Total Pop. = 5,272,000 Mulim Pop. = 87%

Bilo Russia   **Georgia**   **Latvia**

Turkmenistan	Area = 488,000 Sq. Km Total Pop. = 3,856,000 Muslim Pop. = 80%

Ukraine   **Estonia**

Azerbaijan	Area = 86,800 Sq. Km Total Pop. = 7,146,000 Km Muslim Pop. = 80%

Kyrgyzistan	Area = 198,000 Sq. Km Total Pop. 4,506,000 Muslim Pop. 82%

Russia

Kazakhstan	Area = 2,717,000 Sq. Km Total Pop. = 16,943,000 Muslim Pop. 62%

Muslim majority republics within Russian Federation

Tartaristan	**Bashkirah**	**Daghistan**	**Checheno Ingushetia**	**Chuvash**
Area = 6,800 Sq. Km Total Pop. = 6 million Muslim Pop. = 85%	Area = 143,000 Sq. Km Total Pop. = 4.25 million Muslim Pop. 82%	Area = 143,000 Sq. Km Total Pop. = 2 million Muslim Pop. = 85%	Area = 194,000 Sq. Km Total Pop. 1.75 million Muslim Pop. 90%	Area = 19,000 Sq. Km Total Pop. = 1 million Muslim Pop. = 70%

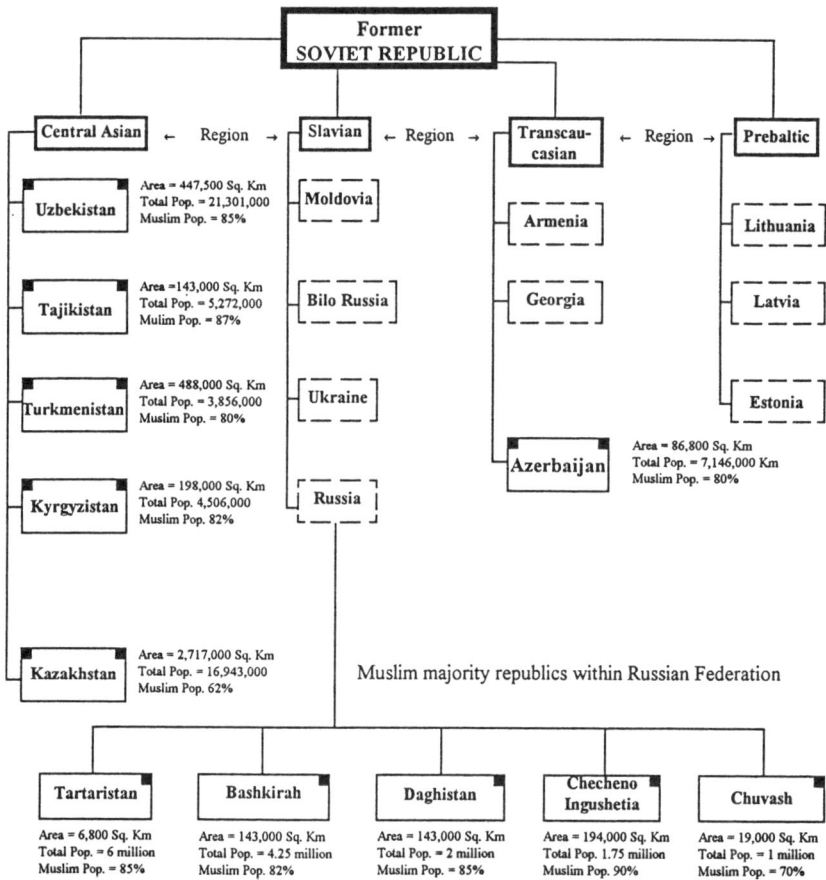

Islam in Central Asia and Russia

Islam in Spain

History provides Muslims from their past some useful lessons that should enable them to analyse their present and plan for the future. The ups and downs in the fortunes of Islam from the panorama of times past re-affirm the validity of principles and predictions enshrined in both the Qur'an and the *sunnah* concerning not only the rise and fall of nations in general but also the reasons for Muslim's own rise and decline. It is also a useful reminder of what mistakes the Muslims made in the past and how they suffered because of it.

History of Muslim Spain is an example from which many lessons can be learnt for the present and the future. It represents a period of Islam covering almost 700 years. We shall briefly look at this period of Muslim rule.

The first conquests of Spain or the area of Spain known to Muslims as Andalusia began in 711 CE (92 AH). Andalusia was part conquered by Tariq ibn-Ziyad a freed man of Musa Ibn Nusayr who was governor of the Muslims in North Africa based in the city of Qayrawan in the region now known as Tunisia. This was under the *khilafa* of al-Walid ibn Abdul-Malik in Damascus.

It is said that while the Muslim fleet was sailing across the sea from Africa to Andalusia Tariq ibn-Ziyad saw in his dream the Prophet Muhammad (SAAS) who said: 'Take courage O' Tariq and accomplish what you are destined to perform.' Tariq anchored close to what is now known as Gibraltar and which was known by Muslims as *Jabl-e-Tariq*. And he accomplished what he was destined to perform.

From the commencement of this foot-hold conquest Muslims expanded and ruled over Spain for a period of nearly 700 years. This was one of the most glorious periods of Islam and also, at the end of it one of the most tragic. And it is for this reason that we have included Spain in our short essays. Here are the lessons of history:

1. Muslims conquered Spain to spread the religion of Allah (SWT) into an area of Europe which was ignorant, feudal, backward and absolute hell for anyone who was not Catholic. It was particularly hellish for the Jews who were being mercilessly persecuted.

2. They ruled on the basis of justice, with no compulsion in religion. The majority of their subjects included Christians who were Catholics and they were not only allowed to practice their religion but the sanctity of their churches and institutions, property, personal honour and safety were guaranteed.

3. The Jews who were being mercilessly persecuted for many centuries previously found for the first time not only peace and security but complete freedom to practice their faith as well as their profession and vocation. It is the descendents of the same Jews who are now active in plotting against Muslims on a world-wide scale.

4. The Muslims flourished in Spain for several hundred years and Spain reached new heights of civilisation, culture and learning in all fields of human activity and endeavour.

Then began the decline of Muslims on two fronts; firstly their own perversity, wrong doing and deterioration of their faith in Allah (SWT) and lack of practice of Islam; and secondly their disunity.

Their disunity among their own ranks was so much that despite the threat of the enemy they fought with one another enlisting the aid of the Spanish Catholics. They continued to fight and weaken themselves until one by one their various small kingdoms were lost and finally Abu Abdullah the Caliph of Granada capitulated to the Catholic army led by Ferdinand in January 1492 after a siege lasting seven months.

And so after 750 years when the Muslims first landed in Spain they relinquished the last of their management and got out of it.

There then followed the most brutal destruction of every Muslim institution, Muslim heritage and every conceivable atrocity against their person, including their forced conversion to Christianity. The Jews too were expelled from Spain, and all Muslim libraries, mosques, schools, universities, institutions were totally destroyed by the Catholics. And these were the same Catholics who were accorded complete religious freedom of worship and security for their churches by the ruling Muslims.

The above is a clear lesson which demonstrates that Muslims will always prosper as long as they follow the book of Allah (SWT) and practice His Commands. This is a basic lesson to be learnt not only form their history in Spain but also their history from the recent past. Whenever the Muslims ignored the Prophet's (SAAS) warning in his last sermon not to let go the book and his *sunnah* the consequences for them have been disastrous. The message of this can be summed up in a sentence: As long Muslims have faith and are virtuous they will remain in ascendency, no sooner their faith and their virtue starts declining they start their downward slide. This is the gist of the lesson that repeatedly strikes whenever Muslims look back at their past history. It is also what applies today and will apply in the future.

Alhamdulillah, after nearly five hundred years of extinction of Muslim rule one of the biggest mosques in Europe is now in Spain, built recently. Conversion to Islam is now taking place in Spain particularly in Granada region as more and more Spanish people realise and recognise the majesty and simplicity of Islam.

Alhamdulillah: All praises are due to Allah (SWT) alone.

Muslim Countries of the World

With the break-up of the Soviet Union there are now nearly 60 countries in the world with a Muslim majority. Among them are some of the poorest to some of the richest in terms of GNP. A common feature of the Muslim countries is their backwardness and lack of influence on the world scene. They make up 30% of the membership of the United Nations, but in terms of political influence in the world their percentage on the scale of influence is very low. This is even lower in terms of economic and scientific influence. In terms of military influence alone it can safely be said that their influence in the New World Order is almost nil.

The reason for this is their lack of industrial, technical, scientific and management development, combined with their failure to establish efficient representative governments.

It is sad that most Muslim countries do not have stable and just governments, proper strategic thinking and development planning, higher educational institutions and advanced research establishments. Many are perennially preoccupied in power politics and full-time exploitation, others have on their mind nothing but survival at the top at all costs. Many readers of this book will readily identify those countries.

Because of their manpower, material resources and strategic spread in the world, Muslim countries have a lot to contribute both individually and collectively to the moral, cultural, economic and spiritual welfare of all the people on earth not just Muslims.

Some of the newly independent Muslim countries of Central Asia have great potential for agricultural development. Their contribution in scientific and other fields could also be significant. There are of course many difficulties in their settling down period but the future looks bright for them.

The dynamism of South East Asian countries of Malaysia and Indonesia and their rapid development augurs well for the future and should be an example to other Muslim countries.

In addition to the Muslim majority countries listed here there are Muslims in minority in almost every country in the world. The most significant Muslim minority country is of course India which has a Muslim population of over 100 million making up nearly 12% of the total population. China, Europe, America and many countries in Africa have significant Muslim population. The current Muslim population in the world is well over 1,000 million. Despite the absence of any well organised missionary work there is rapid conversion to Islam as more and more people in the West are beginning to realise the majesty, simplicity, logic and practical applicability of this religion and way of life to our world.

To regain their lost power and influence and to be able to contribute once again to the science, culture and civilisation of the world Muslim must do the following:

G Increase their faith in and awareness of Islam both in theory and practice, both individually and collectively on a global scale. Some call it Islamic renaissance but it requires no label.

G Govern themselves on Islamic principles by setting truly representative Islamic governments. Getting rid of dictators and tyrant rulers is every Muslim's religious and moral duty.

G Unite or at least NOT fight or harm each other.

G Develop themselves   educationally, technically, scientifically, industrially, managerially as a matter of urgency.

G Muslim writers, thinkers and good Muslim governments must re-assure all and particularly the Western people and governments that terrorism,tyranny and fundamentalism have nothing to do with Islam.

Muslim leaders and those who are in positions of influence should reflect on the teachings of Qur'an and *hadith,* and on causes and effects in past history. They should do so in conjunction with the principles of common sense, logic and strategy.

Until Muslims seriously think and implement the above urgently their future could well be even more bleak than their present and recent past. **And they will have only themselves to blame!**

The following *aya* explains this clearly.

"... Verily, Allah does not change men's condition unless they change their inner selves; and when Allah wills people to suffer evil [in consequence of their own evil deeds], there is none who could avert it: for they have none who could protect them from Him."

(Surah Raad 13:11)

The tables show the Muslim countries of the world together with some basic information.

MUSLIM COUNTRIES OF THE WORLD

Country	Region	Area (Sq. Km.)	Capital	Government	Population	Percentage of Muslims
Afghanistan	South West Asia	652,090	Kabul	Republic	10,000,000	99%
Albania	Europe	28,748	Tirana	Repbublic	3,080,000	75%
Algeria	North Africa	2,381,741	Algiers	Dictatorship	22,971,500	96%
Bahrain	Middle East	688	Manama	Sheikhdom	443,200	98%
Bangladesh	Asia	143,999	Dhaka	Republic	110,000,000	85%
Brunei	South East Asia	5,765	Bandar Siri Beginan	Sultanate	221,900	70%
Cameroon	West Central Africa	465,054	Yaounde	Dictatorship	9,880,000	55%
Central African Republic	Central Africa	622,984	Bangui	Dictatorship	2,775,000	55%
Chad	North Central Africa	1,284,000	N'Djaminae	Republic	5,018,000	80%
Djibouti	East Africa	23,200	Djibouti	Republic	337,000	90%
Egypt	Meditaranian Basin	1,002,000	Cairo	Parliamentary Republic	49,560,000	92%
Ethiopia	North East Africa	1,221,900	Addis Ababa	Republic	46,000,000	65%
	(At the time of writing this book, Ethiopia was engaged in Civil war).					
Gambia	West Africa	11,295	Banjul	Republic	695,000	85%
Guinea	West Africa	245,857	Conakry	Republic	6,075,000	95%
Guinea- Bissau	West Africa	36,125	Bissau	Republic	890,000	70%
Indian Ocean Islands	Indian Ocean	Covers Comoros, Maldives, Laceadives, Zanzibar			1,130,000	99%
Indonesia	South East Asia	1,904,569	Jakarta	Republic	187,000,000	90%
Iran	Middle East/ Central Asia	1,648,000	Tehran	Islamic Republic	49,860,000	98%
Iraq	Middle East/ West Asia	434,925	Baghdad	Dictatorship	17,090,000	94%
Ivory Coast	West Africa	322,463	Yamoussoukro	Republic	10,056,000	55%
Jordan	Middle East/ West Africa	97,740	Amman	Parliamentary Monarchy	2,910,000 (exc.West Bank)	95%
Kuwait	Middle East/Persian Gulf	17,819	Kuwait	Sheikhdom	1,986,000	98%
Lebanon	Eastern Mediterranean	10,400	Beirut	Parliamentary Republic	2,668,000	58%
Libya	North Africa	1,759,000	Tripoli	Republic/ Dictatorship	3,500,000	98%
Malaysia	South East Asia	330,434	Kuala Lumpur	Parliamentary Monarchy	16,921,300	54%
Mali	West Africa	1,240,000	Bameko	Republic	8,206,000	90%

Country	Region	Area (Sq. Km.)	Capital	Government	Population	Percentage of Muslims
Mauritania	North West Africa	1,030,700	Nouakchott	Republic	2,010,000	99%
Morocco	North Africa	446,550	Rabat	Monarchy	27,000,000	99%
Niger	West Central Africa	1,267,000	Niamey	Republic	6,317,550	95%
Nigeria	West Africa	923,768	Lagos	Federal Republic	110,000,000	65%
Oman	South East Arabia/ Middle East	300,000	Muscat	Monarchy (Sultanate)	1,276,000	99%
Pakistan	South West Asia	796,095	Islamabad	Republic	102,200,000	97%
Palestine	Land at the Eastern end of the Mediterranian Sea. Now the Jewish state of Israel. Since 1948 the Palestinians have been a people in search of a homeland.					
Qatar	Persian Gulf/ Middle East	10,000	Doha	Sheikhdom	450,000	100%
Saudi Arabia	South West Asia/ Middle East	2,200,000	Riyadh	Monarchy	16,520,000	100%
Senegal	West Africa	196,192	Dakar	Republic	7,740,000	95%
Sierra Leone	West Africa	71,740	Freetown	Republic	4,100,000	65%
Somalia	East Africa	637,657	Mogadishu	Republic	8,111,000	99%
	(At the time of publication of this book Somalia was engaged in Civil war).					
Sudan	East Africa	2,505,800	Khartoum	Republic	25,150,000	85%
Syria	East Mediterranean	185,180	Damascus	Dictatorship	12,471,000	88%
Tanzania	East Africa	945,050	Dodoma	Republic	26,070,000	65%
Togo	West Africa	56,785	Lome	Republic	3,566,000	55%
Tunisia	North Africa/ Med Coast	164,150	Tunis	Republic	8,094,000	95%
Turkey	Eastern Mediterranean	779,452	Ankara	Parliamentary Republic	56,549,000	99%
United Arab Emirates (UAE)	South East Arabia/ Persian Gulf	83,600	Abu Dhabi	Federation of Sheikhdoms	2,250,000	100%
Upper Volta	-	275,250	-	-	6,000,000	55%
Yemen	South Arabia/ Red Sea	528,000	Sana	Republic	11,750,000	99%
Xinjiang (East Turkestan)	People's Republic of China	-	Urumqi	Autonomus Status with PRC since 1955	13,500,000	60%

MUSLIM COUNTRIES IN FORMER SOVIET REPUBLIC
(BASIC INFORMATION ONLY)

Country	Region	Area (Sq. Km.)	Capital	Government	Population	Percentage of Muslims
Uzbekistan	Central Asia	447,500	Tashkent	Ind Republic	21,301,000	85%
Tajikistan	Central Asia	143,000	Dushanbe	Ind Republic	5,272,000	87%
Turkeministan	Central Asia	488,000	Ashkabad	Ind Republic	3,856,000	80%
Kyrgyzistan	Central Asia	198,000	Frunze	Ind Republic	4,506,000	80%
Kazakhstan	Central Asia	2,717,000	Alma-Ata	Ind Republic	16,947,000	62%
Azerbaijan	Trans Causasian	86,800	Baku	Ind Republic	7,146,000	80%

THE FOLLOWING ARE MAJORITY MUSLIM REPUBLICS WITHIN THE RUSSIAN FEDERATION

Country	Region	Area (Sq. Km.)	Capital	Government	Population	Percentage of Muslims
Tartaristan	Slavian/Russian	6,800		Republic	6,000,000	85%
Bashkira	Slavian/Russian	143,000		Republic	4,250,000	82%
Daghistan	Slavian/Russian	50,000		Republic	2,000,000	85%
Checheno/Ingus	Slavian/Russian	194,000		Republic	1,750,000	90%
Chuvash	Slavian/Russian	19,000		Republic	1,000,000	70%

Islam and Some Current Issues

There are many current issues affecting Muslims. The injustice and tyranny that is being inflicted on ordinary Muslims will have profound consequences for all of us. They also confirm the view held by many ordinary people that when it comes to their 'National Interest', Western governments are capable of despicable acts both directly or indirectly to safeguard them. The notion of justice, fairness and decency have little or twisted meanings. The monopoly of Western powers on world institutions is used to legitimise any unjust act. For known and unknown reasons Muslims at present seem to be at the receiving end of this New World Order treatment. Let us look at some issues:

A. Bosnia & Hercegovina.

So much has already been written and reported in the last eighteen months on Bosnia before the publication of this book that we will bore our readers by writing the same. But injustice and inhumanity on such a large scale, deliberately allowed to go on by the leaders of Britain, France and ECC are so offending and shocking that men of conscience will always protest against it by words and deeds. Here is a letter printed in the August 28 issue of the prestigious international news magazine 'The Economist' that speaks for many:

'Sir- In Sarajevo (August 7th) we are witnessing the death of justice and fair play in international relations. If even a tenth of such atrocities had been committed by a Muslim country against a Christian country or against Israel, the military strength of America, Britain, France and others would have jumped into action.' Chicago Zia Ahmed.

A further letter appeared in 'The Economist' in its September 18th to 24th issue which is reproduced below. It shows the audacity and pettiness of John Major and his minister of state at the foreign office Douglas Hogg. It is indeed a measure of the very high standards of journalistic and editorial integrity on the part of Economist that this letter was published by them.

Britain and Bosnia

SIR—Last year, Abdul Malida, I and several other British Muslims were involved in the production of a video, which showed evidence of atrocities in the former Yugoslavia. Parts of this video have been seen on television in several West European countries, including Germany, but not Britain. Recently, Mr Malida, after making copies of the video so that the material in it could be more widely available, was visited by the police in connection with the law on the distribution of films of "vice and pornography". The material shows terrible suffering but the only vice in it was perpetrated by Serbs and Croats.

We have sent copies of the material to the prime minister and to Douglas Hogg, minister of state at the foreign office. Mr Hogg, in his reply, refers to "allegations" of mass rape. How is it possible that a minister in the British government can still talk about "allegations" when it is known where the rape camps are, and how many of the victims of this policy—maybe 30,000 or more—are now giving birth to children that no one will want? The prime minister, in his reply, points out that "Mr Malida's video does not give the names of victims or perpetrators . . . If [he] can provide this information, we could forward the tape to the UN." This is like asking the victims of Nazi death camps to name their tormentors before they are believed. How can you ask a 12-year-old girl "who are the 20 men who raped you before killing you?" How can our government write such a letter of indifference? And how do you think British Muslims now view this democratic government?

MOHAMMED
Birmingham   YUSUF MAHMOOD

This letter and its reply tell everyone in no uncertain terms what a decline has taken place in the morals and conduct of those who until now have been beating the drum of civilisation, democracy, justice and liberty. Bosnia has removed the last veil of these pretensions and any vestiges of supremacy of British civilisation as the apex of human aspiration and achievement is now buried with it.

We reproduce on the next page another letter from John Major which also appeared in other publications. This letter sums up the thinking, the strategy and the policy of his government. The same applies to many unjust and short sighted leaders and some narrow minded Christian institutions of Europe. The impotence of Muslim countries not to have put their foot down on the Bosnia issue will be recorded in the history books as one of their most shameful and regrettable acts.

The acts of courage and kindness shown by many ordinary people on this issue is too numerous to mention but it must give some hope to ordinary Muslims to continue with their campaign, pressure and protest until this matter is satisfactorily resolved. Muslims sincerely believe that ordinary people in the West who have done so much will continue to show care and concern for Bosnia victims and other peoples in similar situations. Muslims believe and must continue to believe in what the following Qur'anic verse tells them about ordinary Christians;

"... and you will surely find that of all people they who say:
'We are Christians', are closest to feeling affection for
those who believe. This is because there are worshipful
priests and monks among them, and because they are not
arrogant."
(Surah Maidah 5:82)

We hope that the Majors, the Hurds, the Mitterands and the Clintons, as well as the impotent Muslim leaders realise the gravity of their in-action against the Chetnic crusade and make up for it for the Muslims of Bosnia or they may rot in hell for ever. Above all Muslims in Bosnia and elsewhere must put their absolute trust in Allah (SWT), must realise the importance of not neglecting faith and practice of their religion which is the only safeguard against such trials for them.

IO DOWNING STREET
LONDON SWIA 2AA

THE PRIME MINISTER   2 May 1993
Douglas Hogg
Foreign and Commonwealth
Office
London SW1A 2AH

Dear Douglas
Thank you for your indepth report on the current as well as past situation in the
"Bosnia-Hercegovina" region of the former Yugoslavia.
As you are well aware from previous discussions, both within the "Cabinet" and at
other times Her Majesty's Government has not changed its position on any of the
following policies:

1) We do not agree now or in the future to "arm or train" the Muslims within Bosnia-
Hercegovina with military hardware.
2) We will continue to help impose and enforce the U.N. embargo on weapons to this
region. While we are well aware that Greece, Russia and Bulgaria are supplying arms
and training to Serbia and Germany, Austria, Slovinia and even the Vatican are doing
similar efforts on behalf of the Croatian and H.V.O. forces within the region, it is
of paramount importance that we make sure that no such efforts are successful on
behalf of the Muslims within the region. from Islamic States and Groups.
To this end and until the final outcome of the situation on the ground i.e. the
dismemberment of Bosnia-Hercegovina and its destruction as a possible "ISLAMIC STATE"
within Europe which will not be tolerated, we will continue to follow this policy.
Further, the mistake of training and arming the Afghan fighters against the forces of
the former USSR and their becoming so-called "Islamic Fighters" now in other parts of
the world, as in Bosnia-Hercegovina, will not be repeated with the Muslim population
in Bosnia-Hercegovina. This could lead to serious problems in the future within the
emigre Muslim population within the E.C., and North America. Please see attached paper
from the United states entitled: "Iran's European Springboard?" Dated September 1
1992. Within reason these criteria are becoming more and more relevant, therefore,
special attention by our internal security services should be placed on the Muslim
Communities within the Western States, especially here in the U.K.,
3) Until the situation in the former Yugoslavia is settled we must at all costs make
sure that no state that can be deemed "Muslim" is allowed any say on the West's policy
actions in this area, especially that of Turkey. It is therefore, necessary to
continue with the sham of the "Vance-Owen" peace talks in order to delay any such
possible action until Bosnia-Hercegovina no longer exists as a viable state and its
Muslim population is totally displaced from its land.
Whilst this may seem a hard policy I must insist with you and the policy makers
within the F.C.O., and the Armed Services that this is infact "real-politic" and in
the best interests of a stable Europe in the future, whose value system is and must
remain based on a "Christian-Civilisation" and ethic. This view I must inform you is
also felt in every other European and North American government, therefore, we will
not intervene in this region to save the Muslim population or push to lift the arms
embargo on them. The Muslims in the West must be made to see that they can not oppose
our view of the world in the "NEW World Order" and that by the inaction of the "So-
called" Muslim governments of the world, in doing nothing to oppose the destruction of
the Muslims of Bosnia-Hercegovina and not follow through on their pledges to do
something by the 15.1.93 at the OIC Conference, if the West did not rescue the
Muslims, they are totally powerless to oppose us, as we control their governments.
Whilst I know you do not feel fully as I or the Minister for Defence feel on this
subject, it is important that we all show a united front to those in Parliament and
the country on this matter, especially after the "forceful" attack on this policy by
the former Prime Minister.
I expect all those that serve this government to obey "Cabinet Responsibility!"

Yours sincerely
John M.

B. The Palestinian Problem.

This is another thorny problem left behind by the departing British and the half actions of United Nations that has inflicted such terrible suffering and injustice upon such a large number of people.

For the past fifty years the Palestinians under mercurial, emotional but incompetent leadership allowed themselves to be used as a football, with both the Israelis and the Arabs providing the players to kick them on the playing fields of Middle East politics. Palestinians have been used, abused and suffered to serve this or that cause of this or that Arab dictator. Israel has used and sometimes was forced to use 'The TURTLE Tactics' as well as the 'Fist of ZION,' against the Palestinians. We are of firm opinion that a peaceful solution is in the best strategic and long term interests of both Israelis and Palestinians and in keeping with reality. We see a successful peaceful settlement possibly resulting in the following scenarios:

i. Peace and economic prosperity for Israel.

ii. Peace, development and better living conditions and general advancement for Palestinians.

iii. Full recognition of Israel and better relations with its Arab neighbours. This co-operation may result in Israeli technical assistance for the development of Arab economies and technology. Whether one likes it or not Israel is very advanced technically particularly in desert agriculture and salt to fresh water conversion technology and has much to offer to its Arab neighbours.

iv. It will result in the demise of dictatorial and tyrant rulers of Middle East and Africa and will ensure further security for Gulf Rulers.

v. There is every reason to believe that Israel will agree and even help Palestinians to have a full-fledged state of their own in return for USA or internationally guaranteed defence and security pack between them. An era of great peace and prosperity may dawn on this important region.

Any strategy that leads to peace and harmony between peoples is preferable to confrontation and those who oppose peaceful settlement between Israel and the Palestinians are short-sighted and ignore reality and strategic thinking.

If Israeli deception or Palestinian disunity results in no peace or a resumption of conflict after peace has been signed then the prospects for both the Israelis and the Palestinians will be grim indeed. All other Middle Eastern countries will be affected as well.

There is an additional strategic consideration. Israel is now the sole driver of its peace train. When all the Arabs and those who have not yet established relations with Israel are on board this train the Palestinians may be ditched or asked to pay first class fare for a third class trip. This is a strategic scenario and a possible Israeli trap for which the Palestinians should get their Think Tanks working overtime. There are strategic, diplomatic, defensive and propaganda moves that the Palestinians must set in motion to remain as first class passengers on the Israeli peace train until the journey's end.

C. Kashmir.

Another legacy of Britain left behind after partition of the Indian sub-continent. The atrocities that are being committed here by the soldiers of Hindu India to this Muslim majority state is beyond description. If an urgent solution is not found quickly and if the atrocities continue then the only solution that we can think of is for Pakistan to open its borders and allow one hundred thousand Afghan and Pathan *mujahedin* funded by Gulf countries to help the innocent men, women and children of Kashmir and to give the Indian army a piece of their own medicine. Because of 'our National Interest', no one should count on any help from Britain or ECC for the beleaguered Kashmiris.

D. West and repressive Muslim regimes.

This includes help given by France to the repressive regime
of Algeria. And American encouragement to Mubarak to
terrorise the Egyptian people. Our advice to them is: 'Keep
off because that will be better for you.' Once Muslims have
taken the struggle against tyranny in their hands no power on
earth can help and prop any tyrant ruler over them. These
Muslims are fighting a just war for justice, liberty and a
lawful government. Sooner or later these repressive regimes
will fall and better governments must be established.

In many situations concerning Muslims the West
particularly Europe adopts different standards. It may think
it is being very smart but it is not. Economic power is
moving from Europe to Far East and South East Asia and
this in the near future will be followed by Middle East.
Britain may find herself getting a luke-warm welcome in
many Muslim countries in future because of her recent
conduct. The current British/Chetnic partnership cannot be
very profitable for Britain's long term interests.

E. British Governments unjust treatment of Muslim School Children.

There are three hundred thousand Jews in Britain and they
are probably its wealthiest citizens. They have twenty one
Jewish schools state-funded by the British government. In
addition two thousand Anglican and two thousand Catholic
schools are also state-funded by the government. There are
over two million Muslims living in Britain. The efforts of
Islamia primary school to be the first Muslim school to
receive state-funding has been deliberately frustrated by the
British government for the past few years. This is a gross
injustice to and discrimination against the Muslim
community of Britain. Because of the importance of this
issue and the injustice inflicted on Muslims by no less than

Her Majesty's government we believe that this fight should not only be carried on but stepped up.   The support of all Muslims and other fair minded citizens of whatever religion and background must be mobilised. The case must be taken to the European Court of Human Rights and a mass campaign by Muslims in UK along the following lines should be initiated:

a. Media campaign and any further appeal to UK courts.

b. Writing to all MP's, members of House of Lords, prominent educationists and any one in positions of influence.

c. Writing to all Muslim Embassies pointing out the injustice being meted to British Muslims.

d. Writing to all Muslim governments and Muslim education ministers pointing out British governments conduct.

e. In addition to appeal to European Court of Human Rights any other appeal or court case that can be proceeded with in say ECC, United Nations, here in UK must be initiated at once.

f. A fighting fund must be set up and all Muslims must contribute to it. Possibility of obtaining legal aid or grant from any charitable foundation should be also be explored.

g. Volunteer Muslim workers must offer their services free of charge at the campaign headquarters, part or full time.

The Richest Muslim Country in the World

No doubt you guessed from the title that it is Saudi Arabia. We cannot blame you because we thought the same until we looked into it. And we made a shocking discovery, three in fact. The richest Muslim country in the world is not Saudi Arabia (in fact it is quite poor); America is no longer the richest country in the world; the richest country in the Middle East is Israel!

GNP - gross national product is defined as the total market value of the final goods and services produced by a nation's economy during a specific period of time, usually a year. Gross national product is a convenient indicator of the level of a nation's economic activity. The greater the GNP the richer the country or that is how most of us understand it. But there are other conclusions that can be drawn from it. Say we have two countries called Qamar and Shams. Qamar has so much gold it is coming out of its ears but not much else. According to the geologists Qamar has enough gold at the current rate of its export to last it for the next eighty years. And that is all Qamar does; extracts and exports its gold to the world and imports almost everything it needs, necessities and luxuries, from the same countries who buy its gold. Its GNP per head is listed as $10,000 in economic statistics records. Shams has no gold and little natural resources. But it has advanced manufacturing plants, research and technological know-how and a small but highly developed agriculture. It imports raw materials and exports manufactured goods, know-how and some surplus agricultural produce. Its GNP per head is also $10,000. Now you tell us who is the richer country. The one who is selling the diminishing family silver and living off it and will have nothing to show for it after eighty years. Or the one who is selling goods and know-how and whose knowledge and technology is increasing all the time. You guessed it right, the richer country is of course Shams.

Knowledge, technology and know-how are not diminishing but appreciating assets. The natural resources of a country are depreciating assets. In general terms if a country has both resources and technology it will be among the richest, the second richest group will be those with knowledge and technology alone but little or no resources, and bottom of the list will be those who only have exportable but diminishing natural resources. Their GNP is a mirage. There are some exceptions. Japan for instance, a country now richer than the United States of America. It is quite an achievement because Japan has no natural resources whatsoever. In ten years Israel will be the second richest country in the world; they will beat every one except Japan.

The figures in the GNP Table are for 1989. From this it is clear that in 1989 Saudi Arabia was 30% poorer than Israel. In 1992/1993 the situation has gone worse for Saudi Arabia. According to the Evening Standard (a London newspaper) of 26th July 1993 the Saudi Arabian GNP is now the same as London's, about $108 billion. Allowing for inflation, annual growth of GNP, wiping out of Saudi Reserves due to Gulf war this situation is much worse than in 1989. Currently Saudi Arabia's estimated GNP is around fifty percent less than Israel and Israel has everything going for it, while Saudi Arabia has most things going against it.

The Saudi budget of 1992/1993 envisages revenue at SR (Saudi Riyal) 197 billion and expenditure at SR 169.2 billion leaving a budget deficit of SR 27.8 billion. The deficit estimated at 6.3% of GNP is evidence of the deteriorating health of Saudi Arabia's financial position. The kingdom's finances suffered from eight years of financing Iraq against its war with Iran and then spending an enormous amount of money defending itself from Iraq. Some estimates make this sum in the region of 200 billion dollars, all of it wasted and recycled back to Western banks to pay for the equipment and services for the war. With the new sources of oil now available to the West from Russian republics Saudi economy, which is totally dependent on oil may deteriorate further.

Gross National Product (1989)

Country	Population (million)	GDP (US $) Billion	GDP/Capita (1989)	Index Israel=100
Egypt	51.7	31.5	$640	6.7% ■
Jordan	3.9	3.9	$1005	10.5%
Syria	12.1	11.4	$980	10.3%
Israel	**4.5**	**43.0**	**$9,556**	**100.00**
Iran	49.00	62.00	$1,300	13.6%
Hong Kong	5.8	63.00	$10,862	113.7%
Saudi Arabia	**16.52**	**112.00**	**$6,766**	**70.8%**
UK	57	831.00	$14,538	152%
USA	249	5165	$20,763	217%
Japan	**123**	**2812**	**$22,844**	**239% ●**

■　　　Poor

●　　　Richest Country

On the other hand Israeli exports will rise rapidly. This will be achieved by increased Israeli exports to India, China, Vietnam and the Central Asian Republics previously off limits to it. Israeli Aircraft Industries have set up offices in New Delhi and may modernise the Indian Air Force. Israel has advanced desert agriculture expertise and is providing much needed assistance to Central Asian Republics who have severe water problems. No Arab country including Saudi Arabia has anything to offer to Central Asian Republics. Only Malaysia and Turkey can provide them any help.

It is now clear that Saudi Arabia which every body thought was quite rich is in fact very poor. The situation is in fact much worse for the kingdom. Any country that does not have indigenous knowledge in science and technology at an advanced level and does not have indigenous trained scientists, technologists and craftsmen and a strong manufacturing base is poor indeed. This knowledge is not fashionable but the basis of development and self sufficiency. Saudi Arabia despite three times greater population than Israel and having a head start on abundance of wealth has none of this knowledge and know how.

We show the current position of research and technological eminence of Israel over Saudi Arabia. We have also recommended the add on to the current industrial development thinking and culture of Saudi Arabia. Without establishing this minimum research base no true development, self sufficiency or genuine security is **ever possible** for the Royal Kingdom of Saudi Arabia. Indeed we fear for its very survival beyond twenty five years without this technological and scientific policy change. If any consultant or adviser provides an opposite advice to the Kingdom than the one offered by us above then we can say with confidence that the said adviser or consultant is a con and we challenge them to prove us wrong.

Technological & Research Capability
Saudi Arabia Vs Israel

	Area/Item	Saudi Arabia	Israel
1.	Non Technical Research Establishments	2	16
2.	Science Parks (attached to Universities	Nil	6
3.	Electronic & Defence Technology General Research & Technical Centres	Nil	2
4.	Solar Energy Research Institutes	The Solar village project Uyainah, Riyadh. This plant supplies electricity to 4,000 villages.	1 + see below
5.	Advanced Institute of Science for Theoritical and Applied Research independent of any University.	Nil (Saudi Arabia has a large number of PhD's but no scientists of repute and no advanced research institute)	Weizmann Institute of Science: POB 26, Rehovot; f. 1949; incorporates the Daniel Sieff Research Institute (f. 1934); includes 20 research units grouped into 5 faculties (Mathematical Sciences, Physics, Chemistry, Biophysics - Biochemistry, Biology), and a department of science teaching within the Feinberg Graduate School; 300 teachers; 660 graduate students; Founded within a year of the State of Israel coming in existence and named after Israel's first president Dr.Chaim Weizmann.
6.	Literacy	38%	98%
7.	Atomic Energy	Nil	Israel Atomic Energy Commission: POB 7061, 26 Rehov Chaim Levanon, Ramat Aviv, Tel Aviv; f. 1952; advises the Governemnt on long term policies and priorities in the advancement of nuclear research and development; supervises the implementation of policies approved by the Government, including the licensing of nuclear power plants and the promotion of technoogical and industrial applications; represents Israel in its relations with scientific institutions abroad and international organizations engaged in nuclear research and development (Israel is a member of IAEA). The Atomic Energy Commission has two research and development centres: the Nahal Soreq Nuclear Research Centre and the Negev Nuclear Research Centre near Dimona. The main fields of research are: nuclear physics and chemistry, plasma physics, solid state physics and chemistry, optics and electro-optics, reactor physics and engineering, radiation chemistry and biology, metal-lurgy and materials engineering, nuclear medicine and radio-pharmaceutics, non-destructive testing and evnironmental studies. Research and development projects and work with industrial applications include studies in isotopes, radio-pharmaceuticals, medical and solid state lasers, crystal growth, high-tech. materials (including ceramics, ultra-pure electro-optical materials, infra-red glasses), mineral propsecting and the recovery of uranium from phosphates, use of intense sources of radiation in the medical, chemical and food industries, and the engineering and design of equipment for use in highly corrosive environments. The centres also provide national services: radiation protection, production and distribution of radioactive and stable isotopes, molecule and radio-pharmaceutical labelling, high vacuum engineering, training of personnel, information and documentation, etc. Nuclear Research Centre-Negev (NRCN): POB 9001, Beersheba; equipped with a natural uranium-fuelled and heavy water-moderated reactor IRR2-2 of 25 MW thermal. Soreq Nuclear Research Centre: Yavne 70600; f. 1954; equipped with a 'swimming pool' type research readctor IRR-1 of 5 MW thermal.
8.	Nuclear Research	Nil	
9.	Aircraft Industry	Nil	Israeli Aircraft Industries Ltd. designs and manufacturers of military and civil aircraft. Koor Industries Ltd. manufacturers, tanks, missiles and every type of defence and advanced industrial equipment. Tadrivan Israel Electronics Industries Ltd. Civil and military electronics manufacturers.
10.	Defence Equipment	Nil	
11.	Defence Electronics	Nil	

SAUDI ARABIAN Economy, Industry and Research.
The Real Route to Development.

Current as proposed/shown by other Consultants.

Add on suggested by ISDS Consultants.

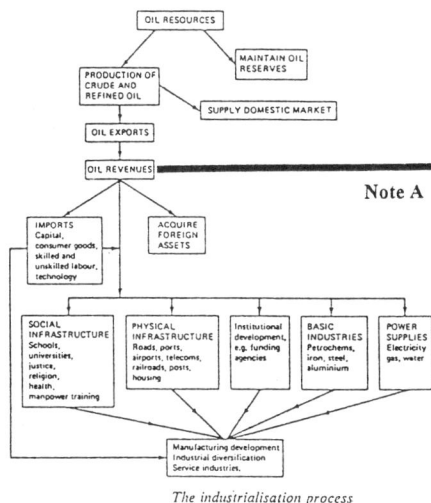

The industrialisation process

Advanced Training Centre for Technician and Craftsmen. All disciplines.	Facility to train 5000 highly skilled technicians per year.
Advanced Desert Agriculture, Desalination, Solar Energy, Animal Husbandry and Forestation Research Institute	200/300 Scientists/ Technologists.
Advanced Institute of Science on the Pattern of Weizmann Institute of Science	500 Scientists/ Teachers and 500 Graduate students.
Advance Research Institute for Manufacturing Systems, Base Metals, Petrochemical, Chemical and Derivatives Research	200 Scientists & Technologists.
Atomic and Nuclear Research for peaceful purposes	200 Plus Scientists 500 Plus Graduate Students.

PLUS

Government owned Manufacturing company/ies for defence, electronics, aircraft and ship building manufacturing.

Note A

Minimum 2% of GNP to be used for research and training independent of present Universities. After the first five years this expenditure on research will start to bring the benefits in substantial savings of imported goods, consultancy and know-how costs, fees and charges.

From this comparison   some   might think that the Saudi's have reached the point of no return and there is no hope for them. Since we have worked as consultants in our individual capacity in the kingdom and also know the research capability of Israel and some Western countries we can say that   Saudi Arabia can become one of the most advanced, technically self sufficient, strong and stable country in the world if it makes the necessary investment in its future and shows grim determination and faith in achieving it.   They have certain advantages that will be further enhanced if they embark on the journey to self sufficiency taking into account our brief comments below.

a. They have the right population and population projection for future.

b. They have land, financial resources and infrastructure.

c. They have an excellent resource in their educated citizens and in their prince and princesses. Many of the prince and princesses are very intelligent.   With proper advanced education   some of them can be in key positions in the research establishments. They will have work satisfaction and know that they are in control of the most precious resource of their country - knowledge. The Saudi scientific knowledge   will benefit other Muslim countries and humanity at large.

Indigenous   advanced technology   will give them a defence strength that no one can challenge.   There is no shortage of Muslim and non-Muslim scientists to fill the needed manpower of the proposed research and training establishments. Control for establishing and running these establishments must be kept under very competent Saudis to ensure the engagement of high quality personnel and regular monitoring so that research and training objectives are met. This is not another usual commission earning opportunity for Saudi merchants or princes to swell their Swiss accounts.

d. We are aware of the self-sufficiency that Saudi Arabia has achieved in many items of food production and is now able to export wheat and some other items. Saudi agriculture is highly subsidised, the cost of production of some agricultural items are nearly three times North American costs. Many Saudi armchair gentlemen farmers make more money from subsidy than from producing and selling in an open market. The need for indigenous advanced research and technology in water conversion, desert agriculture, mechanised farming, farming management is even greater here. Saudi agriculture has vast potential but it must be competitive in international markets. This can only be achieved by reaching the same level of efficiency as the North American farmer which means highly mechanised farming which in turn means advanced research, technology and equipment.

e. At present some of the prince's and big merchant's greatest ambition is to be the biggest importer and biggest commission earner. There cannot possibly be any pride for any self respecting prince or merchant who makes money with such shameful dependence on outsiders where he has to import even toilet rolls for his country.

The Development of Muslim Countries

1. Background.

We have said before as to what is the basic purpose of acquiring knowledge in Islam. It is neither glorification of self nor acquisition of power. The acquisition of knowledge resulting in specialist training and qualification does enable a person to earn a livelihood. However, his basic purpose as an individual is still to serve humanity and all creations of Allah (SWT) in whatever way he can.

A nation or a country is a cumulative sum total of its people. The quality and level of advancement of knowledge of its individuals sees its expression in the development of the state. A backward country is unlikely to have people very forward in knowledge and vice versa. The superiority of some of the Western nations in industrial, scientific and management fields reflect the superiority of knowledge of its individuals.

2. Object and Benefit of Development.

In an Islamic country the basic purpose of development in all fields of industry, science, technology and management is the same as in the West but with some moral and behavioural restrictions. Muslim countries should develop the resources of their country, to meet the needs and aspirations of their people, to provide greater opportunity for trade, to be able to assist less fortunate and less developed neighbours, to become self sufficient and to be better prepared for defence.

It is not correct to assume that because some Muslim countries will become highly developed trade opportunities for the West will decline. Trade increases in a country where there is extensive development activity. Technical and scientific development is a continuing process and is relative to all the countries. As some third world countries develop to the same level as the West is at present say in the next 25 years, one can assume that the West then might still be 25 years more advanced when compared to those third world countries. To close the knowledge and know-how gap is not so easy when the level of knowledge and know-how differs so widely. There is also the possibility that if the third world countries can meet most of the demands for products and services of this world, the West may move its scientific and development activities to other parts of the universe.

It is not beyond the realms of possibility that if by 2050 AD countries like Indonesia, Malaysia, Taiwan and China can meet most of the manufactured goods needs of the Americans much of the advanced factories and the research centres of America might well become busy exploiting the mineral resources of the moon or another planet. This argument has been mentioned because some in the West consider the advanced industrial and scientific development of the third world countries including Muslim countries as a threat to themselves. But this is not so. The development of Japan and Taiwan has posed no threat to ordinary people anywhere or to the economies of other countries. On the contrary it has made possible, for a large number of ordinary people to acquire many useful products at a reasonable cost some of which were previously considered luxuries and could only be afforded by the rich. After all even a poor country like India is being helped by Western businesses to introduce Indians to the pleasures of Coca-Cola, chewing gum, shampoo and tooth paste and to enable them to manufacture their own cars, bombs, tanks, fighter planes and missiles.

3. Why Muslim Countries are Backward in all fields of Industrial, Scientific and Management Development?

Despite their vast natural wealth and the talent of their people many Muslim countries are very backward. Why? One may ask since most of them have now been independent for over 20 to 50 years from foreign rule and in fairness cannot justify blaming America for their backwardness. The reasons are as follows:-

☞ Many Muslim countries have corrupt and incompetent leadership full of toadies at the top.

☞ They lack courage, foresight and discipline.

☞ They do not have representative forms of government. Only in a government where consultation is encouraged and decisions are taken in the national interest, stability and beneficial long term development would be possible.

☞ Majority of citizens and most leaders of many Muslim countries are greedy and have excessive material desires for personal gratification. Instead of building the country's infrastructure, educational establishments, research and technical centres, resources are being diverted to the building of palaces, villas and squandering of wealth in casinos, gambling joints and financing of unproductive and un-Islamic ventures.

↝   The leaders of some Muslim countries have an exaggerated sense of self importance and ego which makes it difficult for them to think clearly or do any meaningful self-analysis as to what is good for their country, what is proper and what is improper.

↝   It is considered honourable by some countries such as Gulf Sheikhdoms to import even corn flakes, soap and every other basic necessity (dependence of the worst order) rather than manufacture some of them locally.   It gets even worse for technical and scientific goods.

↝   The Muslim countries are very disunited and have excessive nation-state nationalism.   This prevents regional co-operation for development.

↝   Many Muslim countries suffer from inferiority complex. This is evident when one travels in some Muslim countries, particularly Arab countries how depressingly and deeply they are impressed with all things foreign, particularly the latest imported gadgets.   The greatest ambition of many Arab businessmen is to be the biggest importer and commission earner. He does not know much about heavy and technologically advanced manufacturing; terms like science parks, advanced industries, research consultancies might give him a heart attack.

4. The Effects of Under Development on Muslim Countries.

4.1 Permanent sense of insecurity/ fear of defeat.

An underdeveloped country can never feel secure against a technologically developed country. Size of country and the size of its population are no longer important since technology has made large manpower inessential for defence or attack. The classic example is Israel which is a small country, less than twenty thousand square kilometres while its Arab neighbours are more than four million square kilometres. The population of Israel compared to its Arab neighbours is in a ratio of one to twenty five. Yet even if all the Arabs unite and fight Israel they are unlikely to win any victory. They were defeated in four successive wars despite overwhelming superiority of arms and manpower. The Arab leaders have been fooling us all by blaming each other or blaming America. The truth is entirely different. They have been defeated and will continue to be defeated in future for the following reasons:-

℘ They have no faith in their cause or faith in their religion or people.

℘ They are incompetent and disunited.

℘ They have no comparable technical or scientific knowledge, none whatsoever in advanced defence industries or advanced research.

℘ No arms industry, heavy machine or manufacturing, spare parts making plant or capability whatsoever exists in any Arab country. It is a cruel joke to say that Iraq or

Pakistan or Iran have atom bombs or missiles. They have no advanced weapons other than what has been given to them by the West or the former Soviet Union. **This applies to all Muslim countries, no exceptions.** Pakistan, Iraq and Iran have been subjected and are still being subjected to suffer from the Zoro Technique, (see the Media and Muslims article). There is no such thing as an 'Islamic bomb'. It does not exist. What does exist and what is reality is 'Hindu bomb', 'Jewish bomb' and, of course, 'Christian bombs', but it is never mentioned as such.

𝄐 They were and still are entirely dependent on outsiders for technical and moral support.

𝄐 They had and still have inferior training, discipline and education. They were and still are solely dependent on foreign powers even for nuts and bolts required for their defence equipment.

In the past these Arabs had some remote chance of winning any war with Israel. Now or in the foreseeable future they have nil chance because for its defence and strike Israel has developed its science, technology and manufacturing capability to such an advanced stage that the Arabs will have a hard job of ever catching up. In fact some Arab countries are sliding backwards rather than moving forward. They have no alternative other than peaceful co-existence with Israel. The sky was thundering in the past until very recently with shouts of pushing the Israelis to the sea from many of these 'Arab heroes from zeroes'. As soon as their bluff was called and reality exposed by Israel they all went quiet like a mouse. The hero of the 'mother of all battles' from Baghdad and the 'hero of terrorists' from

Tripoli have inflicted such wounds on fellow Muslims and Islam both outside and inside their countries that it will take a long time to heal. Once healed these heroes will unleash the same rampage again. You can't teach old dogs new tricks!

4.2 Permanent Instability.
Many Muslim regimes are unstable. Since they are neither good governments nor technically advanced, their instability and vulnerability will remain a permanent feature of their existence. Their citizens despise them for their government's impotence, the *Ummah* dislikes them for their insolence and backwardness; the whole of the West including their so called friends consider them backward, uneducated, lazy and fit only for their resources to be milked.

4.3 They will Waste away their Wealth and Natural Resources.
Some Muslim countries have mortgaged their security to outsiders. They have thus lost control of their wealth as well as true mastery over their affairs. The outsider can and will charge a high price to provide the security. The outsider will also promote conditions to create even more insecurity in such Muslim governments either by encouraging their neighbours against them or by threatening to engineer internal revolt. Not a pleasant situation to be in on a permanent basis! There is no need for us to name those countries that are presently in this terrible catch 22 situation. Some are paying through their nose, others are receiving regular beatings by uncle Sam, some others are under virtual economic siege. No one to blame except the leaders of these countries and of course their country men. Allah (SWT) has clearly said in the Qur'an:

> *"... Verily never will Allah change the condition of a people*
> *unless they change their inner selves ... "*
> (Surah Raad 13:11)

One must feel sympathy with the Gulf countries for being pushed into this situation by the great leader of Iraq. In fact it was a classical application of the 'Batna principle' against them for which they all fell. The 'Batna principle' is explained in our 'The Media and Muslims' article.

5. How can some Muslim Countries rapidly develop themselves into full fledged Industrially developed nations?

Not all Muslim countries can industrially develop themselves to an advanced stage. Some are so poor they cannot even afford the basic infrastructure required for development. Some others have so much ethnic, political and stability problems that they must first sort themselves out. There are a few who will be better off as support economies or purely well developed agricultural economies with only some industry to support more advanced Muslim countries. There are others whose rulers are such a joke that they would not even know what we are talking about.

This still leaves a number of Muslim countries with a potential to become industrially developed in the next 25 to 30 years. Below are our observations on some of them. This list is by no means exhaustive.

In the first group Malaysia has the highest potential of any Muslim country to become a fully developed industrial nation in the next 25-30 years. It has a stable and well managed government, excellent leadership, the sensible policy of gradual introduction of Islamic values and systems into government, and a well thought out plan for development together with a determined and hard working people to achieve their ambition.   It is also a credit to the foresight of the leaders and people of this country to realise that advanced technology, management, education and research are not incompatible with Islam but are the prerequisites to being a good Muslim and a good Islamic country.   Its policy to maintain good relations with all countries and not to be an ally of any extreme group is also in accordance with the teachings of Islam.   Our only advice to Malaysia is to setup as many advanced research institutes as possible along the lines indicated in our essay on 'The Richest Muslim country in the World'.   For a country that is developing very fast it is an absolute must to have an advanced training centre to produce very highly trained and skilled technicians and craftsmen in all disciplines numbering at least two to five thousand qualified trainees a year.   This is a much higher calibre of training than that provided by the local technical college or craft training school or in-house training of employers.

Iran also has the potential provided it can balance its policies of Islamisation with industrialisation. Iran must also urgently set up advanced research institutes and advanced craft training institutes.

In the Second group we believe that Saudi Arabia should be given top priority although it may surprise some people. The kingdom has the high potential to become a very advanced nation in a very short period of time.   Its achievements in the field of infrastructure development and the country as a whole in the last 20 years have been impressive. However, to become a self sufficient industrially developed nation it needs to drastically change its priorities and policies for the next 25 years.   We have discussed this in our essay on 'The Richest Muslim Country in the World'.

Indonesia has the potential but needs further major investment in infrastructure, stable government and long term development plans and policies.

Pakistan too has the potential but is beset with unstable government, mass corruption and exploitation, lack of central planning for infrastructure development. Most of its top businessmen, landlords and politicians are a cancer to Pakistan. Its citizens aspirations are presently fully absorbed in the enjoyment of Western consumer goods at all costs and it would be quite a job to convince its leaders and people to change their psyche. It has serious drug problem with over two million drug addicts and more addicts joining the Pakistan drug club every day. Unless an Islamic state is established urgently in Pakistan, corruption removed and stability guaranteed this country will never fully realise its potential and will slide backwards in the developed nation's league rather than moving forward. The very rapid increase in India's technical and industrial advancement with Western help and Israeli technical assistance in defence and military electronics industries poses serious threats and danger to Pakistan's future security. With the possibility of a future Hindu government and an advanced and developed India, Pakistan's very existence may be at risk.

In the third group Turkey has the dual potential for both industrial as well as agricultural development. Sudan has great potential to become the bread basket for Middle East and Africa if investment in its infrastructure and agriculture is made by richer Muslim countries in some form of joint venture. Central Asian countries have great natural resources and immense potential but we believe that without political stability and good leadership their resources could well end up being exploited by outsiders.

All these Muslim countries need a role model for industrial development. There is none available either from America or Europe. The role model for these countries are Japan and Israel. Until the second world war Japan was not an advanced manufacturing nation. Its technology was mostly restricted to defence industries in the building of ships, war planes and tanks (like Soviet Union). Japanese goods were considered shoddy as late as 1960's. Just look at Japan now in the 1990's! And Japan is a country with no natural resources. The other example is the tiny nation of Israel. In 1948 when the Jewish state was set up it had nothing - no industry, no research, some agriculture but no natural resources. Today after just 45 years it is one of the most advanced countries in the world. Its research capability, technical know how, in all branches of science and technology - all indigenous - is equal to some of the most advanced countries of the West. In certain fields such as electronics and optics Israel is ahead compared to most countries in the West. It is now completely self sufficient in both research and manufacturing in all its defence and attack requirements.

The top ministers of Muslim countries, their advisers, some of them with PhD's from foreign lands will do well to learn from Japan and Israel's strategic and development planning and achievement in the last 45 years. Indeed some of the ministers and their assistants and advisers should take leave of absence or sabbatical from their jobs to study the Japanese and Israeli miracle in depth!

Conclusion.

This short essay is not suitable for a detailed 'how to develop' write up. But we hope that the above two role models should be enough to give a deep insight into how to develop and why to develop.

The consequences of non-development to Muslim countries both in the political as well as economic fields will be enormous. In areas of defence and security they will be suicidal.

THOSE WHO WILL DO NOTHING WILL DO SO AT THEIR PERIL!!!

Muslim Unity in the midst of Diversity

General.
The communists believed that by bringing uniformity of thought and a common system they will induce unity in their own country as well as among nations. They have been proved wrong as the demise and disintegration of their system indicates. The capitalists, represented by West always believed that everyone must follow the Western culture, civilisation and views otherwise they would remain uncivilised and could not belong to the Smith and Jones club of civilised nations. This resulted in the uncontrolled destruction, in the early years of the colonial expansion, of many local peoples, their culture and their customs. This is particularly evident in South America and Africa.

The latest effort of this invasion of ideas through media, education and missionary work is that many people do not know whether they belong to the West or East. In brief they have an identity crisis leading to other crises and problems. This is noticeable in all communities who have integrated to the West or who have adopted Western ways at the expense of their own rich culture and tradition. While Islam in general has taken full care of this problem of unity amidst diversity, some Muslims still suffer from a sense of confused identity. They have either forgotten their Islam or got too assimilated with Western ways and ideas.

Basis of Global Muslim Unity.
The basis of Muslim global unity is the uniqueness of its faith and the priority it places on this unity of the *Ummah* through Divine Commandments and *hadith*.

"And be not like those who are divided amongst themselves
and fall into disputations after receiving the clear signs ..."
(Surah Al-i-Imran 3:105)

This is an exhortation to Muslims to remain united.
There are glaring examples of present day differences of one
man with other man on the basis of colour prejudice and
assumed superiority of one race over the other. This is so
common in America and Europe. The Qur'an addresses this
problem thus:

"And among Allah's signs are the creation of the heavens
and the earth, and the variations in your languages and
your colours; truly in that are signs for those who know."
(Surah Ruum 30:22)

"O Mankind! We created you from a single pair of a male
and female, and made you into nations and tribes, that you
may know one another. Indeed, the noblest among you in
the sight of Allah is the one who is more deeply conscious
of Allah. Behold, Allah is all-knowing, all-aware."
(Al-Hujuraat 49:13)

The Prophet's (SAAS) advice on the subject of unity
and equality of man was of course from the his last sermon.
The relevant extracts are as follows:-

...'you must know that a Muslim is a brother of a Muslim
and the Muslims are one brotherhood'
....'O people, verily your Lord and Sustainer is One and your
ancestor was one. All of you descend from Adam and
Adam was made of earth. There is no superiority for an Arab
over a non Arab nor for a non Arab over an Arab; neither for
a white man over a black man nor a black man over a white
man except the superiority gained through Allah

consciousness - taqwa. Indeed the noblest among you is the one who is the most deeply conscious of Allah.'

In the annals of human history and literature there is no more stirring, more clear a message that comes from a higher authority than this for the equality as well as the basis of greatness for man.

The above is the foundation stone on which the *Ummah's* unity amidst great cultural diversity is based.

When one travels in the far Islamic lands this unity is noticeable. Despite differences in language and culture the Muslim greets with the same international greeting of *Assalamu Alaikum* (peace be upon you). He prays in the same manner, in the same type of mosque and reads the same Qur'an. In doing all this he may not understand a word of his Muslim brother's language but he still feels a sense of brotherhood and belonging. To a Muslim there is no such thing as colour bar nor of bowing or curtseying to a superior man whether a chief priest or an emperor. The Muslim is not allowed even to bow to Muhammad (SAAS) the most exalted of all human beings. He bows only to Allah (SWT) - not to His or Her Majesties. This in itself is a source of unity for the *Ummah*.

Causes of Muslim disunity.

The causes of Muslim disunity is not the *Ummah*. Indeed, the *Ummah* is very united. The chief causes of Muslim disunity are:-

❖ The establishment of a large number of Muslim Nation States.

❖ The proliferation of corrupt, unjust, incompetent and tyrant rulers who are the major source of Muslim disunity.

❖ The failure to establish good governments on the basis of Islam and *sunnah.*

❖ The over dependence of many Muslim governments for security and technology on the West.

❖ Muslim government's incompetence to manage their resources well and their failure to develop advanced science, advances technology, and advanced management with their own people, within their own countries and within their control.

Neither unity nor strength or self sufficiency can be achieved by any Muslim country unless the above root causes are removed or substantially reduced.

It must be made clear that the purpose of unity of the *Ummah* or the Muslim countries or governments is not in the sense of conspiracy against other people, neighbouring governments or the interests of other countries. The purpose of this unity is to ensure development, advancement, mutual defence and assistance and self sufficiency. It is also to use surplus production and technology in the service and welfare of not only other Muslims but all human beings.

Constructive progress and productive welfare is not possible in an atmosphere of conflict and disunity which leads to mutual destruction and waste.

Much grassroots effort is needed to bring about this unity of the governments and progress of the *Ummah.* This can only be accomplished by the combined efforts of Muslims and the assistance of good Muslim governments and leaders.

Muhammad's (SAAS) Last Sermon

History and literature have preserved from our past some of the master pieces of man's sayings. These consist of sayings, speeches and addresses of well known leaders of nations or historic documents which are thought to be so rich in wisdom and stature that they have been carefully preserved in plate glassed, temperature controlled archives. One of the most famous addresses in history, rich in language and in the depth of its wisdom is Abraham Lincoln's (a famous American president) Gettysburg address. Note the concluding words of this address .....

"that this nation (meaning America) under God, shall have a new birth of freedom; and that government of the people, by the people, and for the people, shall not perish from the earth."

Many know and most agree that Abraham Lincoln was a good man and probably America's greatest president. But good old Abe did not realise what his countrymen would be up to after him, in their interpretation of his words regarding government of the people for the people. If he had known this he would certainly have included some very strong words for accountability of the American government and people in his speech. The American government and many American people have taken this concept of government by the people for the people literally as a licence to waste their own and exploit other people's resources, to allow and tolerate most immoral acts known to man and finally to feel obliged to spread their kind of sickness to everyone else in the world. And all this with no accountability, since accountability to Allah (SWT) is already taken out of the system and as the government itself is engaged in some of these activities the question of accountability hardly arises.

There are of course other sermons and sayings as above but they all have some flaw and often don't have timelessness and comprehensiveness.

Now let us look at another sermon widely known among Muslims as 'The Farewell Sermon of Prophet Muhammad'. The message is reproduced here - translation only - as the original was delivered in Arabic.

This sermon, without any doubt, is a masterpiece of wisdom, common-sense and is totally in tune with the human nature. What is more, it touches on areas and subjects which were applicable when they were delivered, will continue to be applicable in future, but more important they are applicable and appropriate to our times now as never before. And let us not forget that the sermon was delivered 1400 years ago!

We examine some pieces from this gem of a sermon of Muhammad (SAAS):

"O people, your Lord and Sustainer is One and your ancestor is one. All of you descend from Adam and Adam was made of earth. There is no superiority for an Arab over a non- Arab nor for a non-Arab over an Arab; neither for a white man over a black man nor a black man over a white man except the superiority gained through Allah consciousness-taqwa. Indeed the noblest among you is the one who is most deeply conscious of Allah..."

Two of the hottest issues of modern times have been addressed here. First is colour bar which is widely practised both in America and Europe and less widely in other parts of the world. The second concerns race superiority such as preached and practised by Hitler in Germany and still deeply ingrained in the character and psyche of many peoples and nations. These issues were boldly faced and vigorously condemned almost 1400 years ago and these teachings are strictly observed by Muslims among whom colour bar is virtually unknown. No mosque in the world is segregated or can bar a Muslim to enter it because of his colour. The opposite is the case in some American churches in the deep south in the United States. There is of course superiority of one man over the other (that all men are equal is a misleading concept) in Islam, but the basis of this superiority is neither any worldly achievement nor status, however great that may be. The basis is **piety, virtue and Allah consciousness.** Whosoever exceeds in this excels in status! The message also dismisses superiority of nations over other nations, or of one sect or group over other sect or group.

"O people! Be conscious of Allah. And even if a mangled Abyssinian slave becomes your leader hearken to him and obey him as long as he establishes and institutes the Book of Allah."

This is the clearest directive that leadership of Muslims is not a hereditary right nor is meant for the most powerful or the most cunning. The main quality is piety and Allah fearing with the strict provision that such a leader can come from the noblest of family or from the ranks of lowly. A further strict provision is that such a leader is to be obeyed only as long as he holds on to the commandments as given in Allah's Book, meaning that he rules justly and in accordance with Allah's Commands. This sermon is also a good indicator of the Islamic belief that the best man or the most important person is not the wealthiest or the most powerful or whiter than white. But he is the most pious man irrespective of his colour or creed.

"Verily, I have left among you something clear which if you hold fast to, you will never go astray after that - the Book of Allah and the Example - sunnah - of His Messenger..."

Noble words and lofty messages are of little use for the day to day guidance and practical instruction of Man. They will inspire and guide some of the people some of the time or all the people at some time but not all the people all the time. If guidance is not comprehensive and detailed and if it is not just and balanced nobody can lead life properly on the basis of sermons.

The questions 'what to do' and 'how to act' confront us daily. It is in answer to this what the Prophet (SAAS) is referring to when he says 'left behind' for Muslims i.e. the Qur'an and *sunnah*. What is more, it is being re-confirmed that as long as Muslims hold on to them they are not likely to get lost in their journey through life as well as in the Hereafter. Muslim past history as well as the present times are proof positive of what could happen on ignoring this advice of the Prophet (SAAS).

The full message is reproduced here for the benefit of the readers. It was delivered, while the Prophet (SAAS) was on Hajj, on the 9th day of Dhu Al-Hijjah 10 AH in the Plain of Arafat, near the mount of Mercy (Jabl-al-Rahmat) and continued the following day at Mina. Two months after his return from this Pilgrimage the Prophet (SAAS) became sick and after a short illness died on Monday 12th of Rabi Al-Awwal in 11 AH - 8th June 632 CE, just over three months after delivering this sermon. It is this reason why this sermon is called 'The Farewell Sermon of Muhammad (SAAS)' or 'Muhammad's Last Sermon'.

Muhammad's (SAAS) Last Sermon

"All praise is for Allah. We praise Him. We seek His pardon and His help and we turn to Him. We take refuge with Allah from the evils within ourselves and the severe consequences of our actions. There is none to lead man astray whom Allah guides aright and there is none to guide man whom Allah misguides. I bear witness that there is no deity but Allah alone without any partners. I bear witness that Muhammad is His servant and His Messenger.

I admonish you, servants of Allah, to be conscious of Allah and I urge you to obey Him.

O people, listen to me as I deliver a message to you for I do not know whether I shall ever get an opportunity to meet you after this year in this place.

O people, indeed your lives, your properties and your honour are sacred and inviolable to you till you appear before your Lord, like the sacredness of this day of yours, in this month of yours, in this city of yours. You will certainly meet your Lord and He will ask you about your actions. Have I conveyed the message? O Lord, be witness!

So he who has any trust to discharge, he should restore it to the person who deposited it with him.

Allah has forbidden you to take any interest (usury). All interest obligations henceforth are to be waived. But your capital is yours to keep.

Be aware, no one committing a crime is responsible for it but himself. Neither is a son responsible for the crime of his father nor is a father responsible for the crime of his son.

O people, listen to my words and understand them. You must know that the Muslim is the brother of a Muslim and the Muslims are one brotherhood. Nothing of his brother is lawful for a Muslim except what he himself allows. So you should not do injustice to or oppress yourselves. O Lord, have I conveyed the message?

O people, it is true that you have certain rights with regard to your women, but they too have rights on you. Remember that you have taken them as your wives only under Allah's trust and with His permission. Do treat your women well and be kind to them. It is an obligation on women that they do not make friends with anyone that you do not approve and it is a further obligation on them to be chaste.

Behold, everything of Ignorance is put down under my feet. The blood revenges of the pre-Qur'anic days of Ignorance are remitted.

O people, verily Satan is very disappointed from being ever worshipped in this land of yours. But he is satisfied to be obeyed in actions of yours you think trifling. So be cautious of him in your religion.

O people, no Apostle or Prophet will come after me and no new Faith will be born.

Verily, I have left among you something clear which if you hold fast to, you will never go astray after that - the Book of Allah and the Example - sunnah - of His Messenger.

O People! Be conscious of Allah. And even if a mangled Abyssinian slave becomes your leader hearken to him and obey him as long as he establishes and institutes the Book of Allah.

Do listen to me. Worship your Lord and Sustainer. Perform your five daily salah. Fast your month of Ramadan. Make pilgrimage to your House - the Kaba - in Makkah. Pay the zakah on your property willingly and obey whatever I command you. Then will you enter the Paradise of your Lord and Sustainer.

Verily, you will meet your Lord and Sustainer and He will ask you about your actions. Do not go astray after me so that some of you strike the necks of others. O Lord, have I conveyed the message?

O people, verily your Lord and Sustainer is One and your ancestor is one. All of you descend from Adam and Adam was made from earth. There is no superiority for an Arab over a non-Arab nor for a non-Arab over an Arab; neither for a white man over a black man nor a black man over a white man except the superiority gained through Allah consciousness - taqwa. Indeed the noblest among you is the one who is most deeply conscious of Allah.

All those who listen to me shall pass on my words to others and those to others in turn; and may the last persons understand my words better than those who listen to me directly."

"Have I conveyed the message?"
"Yes, O Messenger of Allah,"
his Companions all replied.

The Way Forward

This is our forty-second and last essay. A summing up of the message that we have tried to convey and the pointers that we have highlighted in this book should lead Muslims to 'The Way Forward.' We hope that our summing up clears the issues of terrorism and fundamentalism Vs Muslims. We also give our observations in this essay on 'The MUSLIMS and the New World Order,' the title of this book.

→ **The summing up for 'The Way Forward.'**

→ In our 'introduction' we raised the issue of a possible armed conflict between the New World Order and the Islamic World Order predicted by some writers and Think Tank consultants. We totally reject any possibility of this happening. The days of global wars for territory or to establish religious and doctrinal supremacy are over. No country, not even the United States, now has the power to impose unjust solutions, or force its culture or systems by conflict and conquest. The future international conflict or competition will be for the hearts and minds of people and this conflict will only be between the system, market values and culture represented by the New World Order Vs the system, moral values and *taqwa* represented by the Islamic World Order. However, local ethnic, religious and territorial conflicts in many parts of the world will escalate but they are unlikely to involve international participation other than spectators or exploiters.

→ This conflict requires no bullets, guns or bombs. Islam is now the last hope and stand for morality, virtue, justice and moderation. While there is still much good in it the

New World Order represents an unacceptably high level of injustice, immorality, greed, excess and wastage. Islam must declare a war against this, not only for the sake of Muslims but for all inhabitants of this earth. Even the Hindus once renowned for their moderation and religious tolerance and piety have now been badly corrupted and are fast sliding on the downhill run of greed and vice. This is thanks to the Coca Cola, Dallas and Johny Walker culture which is now penetrating the inner sanctums of Hindu society; a totally alien and destructive force for the destruction of 'Mother India'.

→ The West has the committed vision that they have been endowed with a mission of universal redemption. Having failed to win the world for Christ, they started wholesale export of their secular and material philosophies.

→ It is now clear that this attempt by West at universal redemption has resulted in conspicuous consumption, ecological and environmental destruction and unacceptable level of moral degeneration.

→ The philosophically fragmented and dichotomous West has little to offer Islam. Islam's strength lies in its clearly defined unity of faith, its well explained purpose of life and its vigorously expressed distinction between right and wrong. Equally, the West has little to offer to other religions, civilisations and cultures.

→ The naive faith in the pseudo - religion of progress, in the supremacy of Western civilisation as the apex of human aspiration and achievement, is fading fast. The realisation is growing that both the society and the individual on planet earth are now confronted by apparently insoluble and infinite problems. And the Western civilisation and belief are the main architects of these problems.

➜ We believe that the modern mentality characterised by scientism, materialism, rationalism and its apparent hostility to the supranational is approaching collapse beneath the weight of its illusions and inadequacies.

➜ The Western civilisation, therefore, is no intellectual challenge to Islam. The challenge before Islam is how well and how quickly its truth, its cohesiveness, its comprehensiveness, its moderateness and naturalness can fill the gap left behind by the departing Western civilisation. The urgent task before Muslims is how best they can hold on themselves and make others hold on to the rope of Islam let down for them from up High, continue to maintain and improve the connection with their Creator and remain accessible to and beneficiaries of His truth.

➜ The West has lost its usurped authority of discovering and defending its version of truth because it proved unequal to the task. So the future struggle for all our sakes is not just confined to the Balkans, the Middle East, this or that interest. It is between truth and falsehood, balance and imbalance, light and darkness. In brief the struggle from now on is between the New World Order that represents, despite some rich parts, an unacceptable level of immorality, violence, excess, waste and material greed and the Islamic World Order that clearly represents morality, virtue, balance , moderation and piety. Where does the tyrants and dictators belong in this? They do not belong to the New World Order and they do not represent the Islamic World Order. The sooner they are consigned to the dustbin of history the better for all concerned.

→ It is clear from the true understanding of Islamic teachings as explained in this book that Muslims are neither fundamentalists nor terrorists. Any accusation that levels Islam as fundamentalist or terrorist is a load of tosh. A Muslim committing an act of terrorism is driven by similar motives and is guilty of the same crime as a Hindu, Christian or Jew. We do not label Hindu, Christian or Jewish fundamentalist so why label Muslims as Islamic fundamentalists.

↗ **The pointers to 'The Way Forward.'**

↗ Islam offers to the modern man not just a set of solutions to his problems, but a radically different choice of clear direction and known destination with a tried and tested system.

↗ In order that this choice is made both clear and persuasive it is now the duty of every Muslim to provide a visible demonstration of this choice in the shape of working models of the Islamic system at all levels.

↗ Muslims must believe that by becoming better in faith and practice, by setting up Islamic governments and Islamic institutions, by establishing Islamic laws and values for justice, morality, equality, welfare, care and concern they can provide an assured demonstration of this choice for others to adopt and follow.

↗ The grassroots involvement to strengthen their faith and renew its practice, the *jihad* to set up Islamic governments, their determination to develop their countries and its resources and their exertion in *dawah* to spread the truth are the visible demonstration by Muslims of their determination to achieve the stated objectives. They must undertake this task not only for their own welfare but for the welfare of others as well.

↑ 'The Way Forward.'

↑ **The determined and incessant struggle to achieve these stated objectives is 'The Way Forward' for the Muslims.**

"... Verily never will Allah change the condition of a people unless they change their inner selves... "

(Surah Raad 13:11)

I S D S

ISDS- INSTITUTE FOR STRATEGIC AND DEVELOPMENT STUDIES, is a Think Tank that specialises in Muslim affairs and the Islamic world in the areas of advanced scientific, technological, management and related development fields. It also provides solutions to many strategic, logistics and organisational questions confronting organisations, institutions and governments using the practical experiences of its consultants, advanced software and technologies.

Consultant membership is available to any Muslim scientist, technologist, strategist, thinker, leader who can spare a few hours of his time in the service of Islam. They can be from any country in the world. High calibre original thinkers and doers with ability to distinguish the wood from the tree and being able to device implementable and executable programmes may find their association with ISDS intellectually stimulating and satisfying. ISDS welcomes manuscripts of high standard reflecting its aim and objectives which may require assistance with publishing. We have in-house expertise for all stages of publication.

ISDS is a voluntary organisation completely independent of any institution, government or lobby group. Its only source of funding are the income it generates from its publications plus the generosity of Muslims - individuals, corporations and some governments with grants, gifts and donations. Our supporters identify with our aims ant trust us to carry it out.

At present ISDS is located in London. We hold regular strategy sessions of our UK and visiting consultants in very congenial but *halal* surroundings in Whitehall place, a few minutes from Downing Street. When funds are available we propose to set up an office in Washington - the capital of the New World Order.

Any correspondence, criticism, suggestion, enquiry should be addressed to:

Secretary
ISDS, PO Box 3416, London SW19 8BP, UK.